Praise for *Lies In Silence*

Story after story in this firsthand accounting allows us to see the toll that one person's mental illness takes on an entire family.

> — Christine S. 47, TX. Music teacher, mother of a bipolar teen, with bipolar disorder in her extended family.

Lies In Silence *is a well-written, page-turning book about a woman's heart-wrenching journey through a life infiltrated by bipolar disorder. One can easily empathize with her suffering as bipolar disorder intimately afflicts her and her family. SJ Hart appropriately depicts this illness as one that lies dormant until it consumes one's mind, body, and soul.*

This book offers valuable medical information regarding some of the potential triggers of bipolar disorder, and emphasizes the strong genetic etiology of the illness. It illustrates the need for more medical research and better healthcare for the mentally ill and their families.

> — Melissa B. 37. Family physician, mother of two, sister of a bipolar sibling.

This book offers a poignant and often searing account of the burden of bipolar disorder and mental illness on a family experiencing the effects over three generations. The perspectives as a daughter with a seriously mentally ill father, as a mother with affected children, as a wife and a mental health professional who herself suffers with bipolar depression are all woven together.

Mental illness is not simply a private matter. It also has tremendous public health implications, as we know the adverse outcomes when it goes unrecognized and untreated, including increased risk of suicide, failure to achieve socially, emotionally, academically, and economically, and, for some, increased risk of being a victim and/or perpetrator of violence.

As a child and adolescent psychiatrist who provides clinical care, teaches trainees, and works in the public sector, this book powerfully underscores the message of the importance of education about bipolar disorder and behavioral health (mental illness and substance abuse) across the board. Educating healthcare professionals across disciplines, from primary care to mental health specialists, to recognize warning signs, appreciate what is known about risk factors (including genetic vulnerability), triggers, and when to refer for treatment services is critical. Education must go beyond the healthcare providers to others who touch the lives of families. Schoolteachers, counselors, and principals should be educated, so they can gain a better understanding of behavioral health problems. They can then be part of early identification, support interventions, and be better prepared to address the educational needs of a student with behavioral and mental health problems. Other settings and disciplines include police crisis intervention training, faith-based groups, and many others we interact with on a daily basis. Education remains a powerful tool to combat stigma, misunderstanding, misinformation, their causes, and their treatment.

— G.A.E. 54. Child and adolescent psychiatrist, associate medical director for children's services department, family member with mental illness.

This work does not mince words about an illness that rips lives apart, yet gets little sympathy or respect. Families are living and feeling stigmatized, while stressed beyond endurance. This illness has a higher mortality rate than the average cancer, but no one shows up at your door with casseroles or pies during an especially bad bout of symptoms.

Hart's book allows a glimpse of what this genetically passed on illness does to those afflicted, and the families that live with and love them. Without more research and better medications, more healthcare and less stigma, families with bipolar will continue to live half-lives...I know. I live with this every day, with myself, several of my children, aunts, uncles, cousins, and grandparents. Many of them did not make it.

They were part of the statistics of the mortality of bipolar due to suicide. Others lived in spite of their attempts, yet continue living that half-life.

> — Goldie W. 46, WI. Former job placement specialist for the mentally ill, parent of six kids — five with bipolar disorder; five "known" generations of bipolar disorder; family history of alcoholism and completed suicides.

"If you want to understand someone, walk a mile in their shoes." With her book, Lies In Silence, *Hart allows us to do just that: to look at mental illness from the inside out. It's a painful world to enter, but the understanding the reader comes out with makes this essential reading. It's a rare author or filmmaker who is able to do what Hart has done, to let us see the world through another set of eyes and, in so doing, bring us closer to the truth.*

> — P.H. 43, CA. Filmmaker, family history of depression and completed suicides.

The outside world needs to read this psychological family saga in order to know the feelings of pain, loss, sorrow, grief, and hopelessness that families on the inside endure on a daily basis. Learning, understanding, and dedicating more funding and research are the only ways to eliminate stigma.

SJ's writing style is clear, concise, and riveting, as she presents clear visual analogies providing the reader a first person experience. Her compelling story needs to be read on a widespread basis, by both laymen and professionals. Perhaps it will awaken those outside the painful world of mental illness, so they join the fight of finding the way to rid Lies In Silence!

> — Jackie H. 71, NJ. Retired school secretary, mother of a son diagnosed with major depression, aunt/great aunt of several bipolar family members.

Lies In Silence captured my attention from the first page. I could not put the book down once I began reading it. The story is well written, scintillating, and explosive. It takes a subject that is considered taboo and misunderstood, and brings it to life in terms any layperson can understand. I encourage anyone associated with the field of mental health to read it, as it has value as a supplemental reading in the mental health curriculum.

Prepare yourself for an extremely emotional ride, which drives home the point, in multiple ways, of how tragically mental illness is misunderstood. This book helps all professionals and non-professionals launch out of the Dark Ages and open their eyes to the world of genetics and disease.

> — Gary S. 67, PA. Retired professor of biology (30 years), divorced from first wife who suffered from bipolar disorder.

This is by far the most profound, riveting, pioneering, thought-provoking book I have ever read. Lies In Silence *exposes myths perpetuated by years of misinterpretation as well as the sleeping genetics of potential mental illness. It is time for spiritual leaders, mental health professionals, educators, the medical community, genetic scientists, human genome scientists, departments of correction, the juvenile justice system, legislators, the media, parents, and youth to wake up, listen, stand up, and act. Here is a voice crying in the wilderness. Do you have ears to hear? A must read for those who serve/practice in the fields of spirituality and in mental health.*

> — L.C.H. 48, DE. MSW working in the public and higher education and treatment settings, single mother of three, first husband is incarcerated and likely suffers mental illness.

SJ Hart writes vividly of the excruciating journey of one family's futile attempts to outrun, outwit, and, in any way possible, evade Lies In Silence; *a lose-lose exercise.*

Though my family's war has differed slightly, it is classically similar in many ways. This book belongs in the hands of every person in this country, and should be required reading for anyone entering the allied health professions. The stigma is real; it is horrible and scarring. We must all take some responsibility for bringing it to an end.

— Janet O. 51, CT. Medical secretary, suffered since childhood from major depression/anxiety; a daughter with bipolar disorder and a son with an atypical mood disorder and autism, dad with multiple mental health disorders, and siblings suffering from bipolar, depression/anxiety, and/or alcoholism.

As a member of those in the trenches with Hart, I have to say that this book is a must read. While it is painful to read for those of us that live this way, this is a love story written from the heart. SJ spells out clearly and realistically what families deal with 24/7 when mental illness moves in and steals the ones we love.

Take it in small doses and then take it to the streets to everyone you know, in order to educate and enlighten them to mental illness and how it affects families and their loved ones.

— Deb G. 50, NJ. Businesswoman, multiple family members of many generations suffer mood disorders, raising two teens with bipolar.

One reads the cry of pain here through quickly misting eyes. Unfortunately, my eyes have seen this before through such tears. Though the author's bipolar personally has never attacked me, I certainly felt its heat. After my forty-something daughter's hospitalization, her eight-year-old son, my grandson, asked, "Are you my mother's father? Why can't you take care of her?"

All the memories of my grandfather's drinking bouts, my mother's depression, my brother's alcoholism, and another brother's breakdown flooded my thinking; especially the times that I, the "healthy one," felt inadequate and guilty for my inability to help. The author's courageous exposure of her personal and family pain should be especially valuable to those who personally have not experienced the pain, but love those who are in the silent grasp.

> — R.A.W. 72, NJ. University professor, multiple family members of three generations suffering from bipolar disorder.

Excellent depiction of life in a family dealing with bipolar disorder, and the long-term effects it has on each and every member.

> — Ken S. 48, TX. VP for an international transportation services company, father of a teen with bipolar disorder. Spouse has long family history of mood disorders and substance abuse.

I stopped breathing... there was so much that sounded familiar. For the first time in fourteen years I felt that same numbness return. Confusion, fear, seeking to understand, frustration, misdiagnosis, anger, frustration, ANGER!

*   Mental illness had invaded our normal, happy life, and I just didn't know what to call it until now. Nor did I know there were others who suffered similarly or worse dealing with the charred remains of the life we once knew. Lies In Silence is a wake up call to our society and our medical community that brain disorders need more attention, more resources, more understanding.*

> — T.W.S. 46. Music teacher, suffers from major depression/anxiety, family history includes anxiety; wife suffers from schizoaffective disorder; family history of depression and schizophrenia.

This is a powerful, intense, raw account of one family's devastating journey with bipolar disorder. SJ Hart pours her guts and her grief out honestly and desperately. Her pain and loss scream throughout the book, as her life has been decimated by this illness.

I recommend this book to everyone with a mentally ill family member or friend. I also implore all professionals, especially psychiatrists, social workers, and mental health workers to read Lies In Silence. *It is impossible for it not to profoundly and forever impact your perspective on mental illness.*

> — A.F. 43. LCSW in private practice, divorced from mentally ill ex-spouse.

Powerful... Overwhelming... Sad...

When it comes to mental health, it is hard to believe it's the 21st century where we live daily with computers, cell phones, and state-of-the-art technology. Lies In Silence *reminds us that we are decades behind in understanding pertinent information about how mental illness is breeding and taking our children, as we move ahead in so many other areas of medicine.*

Reading Hart's painstaking and gut-wrenching book was difficult but necessary, as it is relevant to all of us. The questions she asks are pertinent. Is there a connection regarding story after story of teenage violence? Why the myths about motive? "He/she was so happy; they were doing so well in school" rather than asking is it untreated mental illness?

It is time we focus on what appears to be a generation with mutating genes, producing younger children acquiring brain diseases, as this is just one accounting of millions of people suffering throughout our country.

> — L.R.B. 49, PA. Marketing and meeting planner, three siblings and five nieces and nephews suffering with bipolar disorder, family history of completed murder/suicide.

While destruction entered SJ Hart's family, it also took up residency at our house, tearing down dreams and our future. There were years of trying to convince psychiatrists and pediatricians that our daughter had genetically inherited this thing called bipolar. Years of being broken down by raging, hallucinations, medicine trials that failed, manic behavior, suicidal ideations, school failures, neighbors who called the police, friends who became distant, hospitalizations, and anguish for a daughter who was slipping from us. Our teen son ran away, never to return home and was not diagnosed with bipolar until becoming father to two children, later identified with the disease as well.

Looking back through my career as a police officer, I can now see where Lies In Silence had its hold with others. So many stories and events come to mind as I think back on situations where a circumstance could have been handled differently, if we had been trained to recognize symptoms of mental illness. Many times I was on the other side of a knife or gun, a raging youth, or encounters with adults cut down from a successful career and family to living on the street and alone. I shared the anguish of fallen police officers... my friends... who were slain by visibly unstable and ill people. Or, police officers who were dealing with illness themselves and took their own life. It wasn't always them. It was us.

Too many times I transported people to jail, when perhaps they needed hospitalization. Too many times seeing so-called successful people who were broken down to the bottom much like Hart's father. It seems a significant amount of police calls for service are driven by mental illness. My heart is saddened and angry for people who could not obtain the medical help needed because none of us knew, or the ones that did weren't telling.

SJ Hart's amazing story of her family represents so many others who share a similar journey. We are crying out to our medical and academic community to listen. Lies In Silence... is a call to action. It is time to unearth the Lies and shatter the Silence.

Hart has an amazing gift of story. I read of her journey through tears as it brought a painful reminder of my own. Her father must be so proud and grateful. She is a master writer with the ability to tell the story through human eyes.

> — Jerri C. IL. Retired police officer and business administrator, two children and two grandchildren with bipolar, two other children being monitored.

Looking for answers sometimes is at best confusing, and one is often left with nowhere to turn but to the aisles of bookstores. Although Lies In Silence *does not offer answers, it is the first book ever to give a painful inside view with this degree of detail of the multi-generational suffering caused by bipolar disorder.*

It offers validation and a powerful, unwavering affirmation to those who struggle alone, never speaking of the symptoms, pain, or tremendous losses. SJ almost pleads for consumers to ask questions, to demand answers, to speak up and courageously paints an accurate and graphic picture of grief, one of the catastrophic legacies of this monstrous disease.

I've devoted more than 20 years of my career helping those affected with mental illness and substance abuse. The more I read, the more I felt taken aback, as many things I held true for so long were challenged in the haunting questions asked over and over. Things taught to me along the way by clinical supervisors, holding positions of authority and the outcome of mentally ill patients:

"Just take your meds and you will be ok. People with bipolar stop taking their medications because they like the feeling of mania. Medications are the answer; we just have to find the right one and that may take time." I had no idea that these commonly held "wisdoms" were not totally accurate until I read this book.

As I read Hart's story, not only did I open my eyes to challenge some of those old ideas, I also felt a sense of shame and humility. I could have been one of those clinicians described in such detail. I was one of those clinicians. I will no longer be one, and all of those that I supervise will read the book as part of their training.

Lies In Silence will wake up professionals in this field and give clinicians a distinct and unforgettable lesson. A lesson in understanding, respect, and recognition. If we ask the right questions and pay attention, perhaps no one has a better description of their symptoms and their suffering than the person right in front of us. Many of us have recommended applying tough love. This is not about tough love. This is about genetics and human beings.

As a brother, a son, and a friend of countless people afflicted with mental illness and substance abuse, I found this book illustrated a stunning depiction of fear, frustration, and the powerlessness that I undervalued until now.

Lies In Silence has the power to help those feeling alone and dismissed. I believe that it is "one voice," that helps all of us to challenge our own stigma, thinking, and judgments, as it did for me.

> — Mike K. 44, DE. MSW, LCSW, clinical director of dual-diagnosis treatment center, brother and son of diagnosed and undiagnosed loved ones.

I thoroughly enjoyed reading this manuscript. It provides an accessible account of the multi generational path that bipolar disorder can take. It spoke to me as a professional, giving me pause to consider my understanding over three decades of practice of the impact of this disorder. I also think this work provides a comforting touchstone for those struggling to manage a disorder that may have overtaken them or their loved ones at different points in their lives. SJ Hart tells a story that covers a wide range of ages, developmental periods, and stages of family life in a style that is illuminating and commands the reader's attention.

> — M.J.V. psychiatrist and professor.

Lies In Silence

**Lessons about Bipolar and Co-Occurring Disorders
Learned through Advocating for
Appropriate Treatment for My Family**

SJ Hart

Issues Press

Issues Press

An imprint of Idyll Arbor, Inc.

39129 264th Ave SE, Enumclaw, WA 98022

Editor: Thomas M. Blaschko

Library of Congress Cataloging-in-Publication Data

Hart, S. J.
  Lies in silence : lessons about bipolar and co-occurring disorders learned through advocating for appropriate treatment for my family / S.J. Hart.
      p. ; cm.
  ISBN 978-1-930461-08-6 (alk. paper)
  1. Manic-depressive illness. 2. Manic-depressive illness--Genetic aspects. 3. Dual diagnosis. 4. Mentally ill--Family relationships. I. Title. II. Title: Lessons about bipolar and co-occurring disorders learned through advocating for appropriate treatment for my family.
  [DNLM: 1. Hart, S. J. 2. Bipolar Disorder--Personal Narratives. 3. Mental Disorders--complications--Personal Narratives. 4. Family Relations--Personal Narratives. 5. Life Change Events--Personal Narratives. WZ 100 H3259 2009]
  RC516.H39 2009
  616.89'5--dc22
                                    2009014015

ISBN 9781930461-08-6

In Memory of

Those who have committed suicide

Those who have committed homicide, their victims and loved ones

Those who have committed grave and life-altering acts toward
themselves and others

Those who fought and lost to

Lies In Silence

With gratitude and deep humility...

To MS:

For generously sharing your creative vision and ideas in a candid manner;

For assisting me in the transformation of my words from mythical metaphors into an authentic reflection of mental illness;

For your interest, your kindness, and your depth of commitment to Lies In Silence.

For discussing and teaching the most important issue in presenting any story: the quality of credibility.

And always most importantly to me, for being a man who keeps his word with no personal agenda.

To FJK:

For the light you offered, respectfully challenging my darkness and my despair;

For your constant effort to understand my heart, my sorrow, and my personal path, while you walk your own;

For developing our relationship, though based on a parallel foundation of solid difference and poignant similarity;

For opening up to a virtual stranger through sharing a story that brought us together in language and loss;

And perhaps, dearest to me, for passing no judgment or wavering in your own faith in spite of the abyss of my own.

Contents

Acknowledgements

To my husband for his loyalty, his patience,
his support and his love.

To my children who suffer daily, with genetics
that have stolen their innocence, their dreams, and their lives.

To my mother-in-law for her endless assistance
in the day-to-day struggle of our new normal.

To my sister and AJ for never saying no.

To my few real friends who reached out to me,
while I was slipping away.

To my S.I.S. who lit the darkness of the storms
with scented candles and held my hand, while I lost
my mind, my children, and my hope.

To all of my book reviewers, with much gratitude,
for affirming *Lies In Silence* and its significant and
timely value, supporting the candid and honest version of
our personal saga.

To the millions of children, adolescents, adults,
and those who love them; may we someday
find relief from our suffering, and the long-awaited
understanding and compassion,
without the constant sting of stigma.

To my mother; for her years of strength and courage
to fight on in spite of tremendous obstacles and
lack of understanding.

And lastly to my father; rest in peace now, dad.

Prologue

Many years ago, at the age of twelve, I was shaken by the first of several unexpected, agonizing jolts in what was to become my surreal and unimaginable life. My personal life journey. Catastrophic jolts that remain difficult to grasp, that lack any reasonable explanation, and that I resist accepting as the reason for my existence.

Looking back now what *lies in silence* was obvious. There had been hundreds, perhaps thousands, of warning signs. The adults in my life were unable to accurately explain the magnitude of our circumstances themselves. In truth, they wanted more than anything to protect us in the misguided way adults sometimes do. And they were never given adequate information to understand or make some kind of sense of the overwhelming burdens we would experience with little to no resources.

Therefore, I lived for decades with a belief system and core identity, later discovering that it was distorted, skewed, and mistaken. A belief system based on a massive illusion, thus creating vulnerability and ignorance. It was a situation that produced a complete lack of awareness of the impending and inevitable catastrophes that would follow, leaving my family and me unprepared for what lay ahead.

This is our family's story — one family's incomprehensible journey.

Some locations and details have been changed to protect privacy and confidentiality. However, the genetics are 100% accurate. The pain is 100% accurate. The multi-generational suffering is 100% accurate, and the majority of the people discussed are real.

Our story is alarming and it is meant to sound warning bells! Loudly! For anyone and everyone who will listen. My family's story is instructive for those who live with or work with the mentally ill. It may touch those who are mentally ill or those loving someone mentally ill. Our collective pain and suffering may sound eerily familiar and resonate for some. As it is in our daily reality, the obstacle we most share is stigma, as many of us typically suffer alone and in isolation. It is easy to recognize stigma from others as it cuts us to the core, but sometimes the stigma from within and the constant feeling we are broken is the largest obstacle to finding our voice and demanding changes.

We live in a world not known to those who exist outside the horror of brain disease. And many non-sufferers judge our world in very public and disrespectful ways.

It is our time to speak and educate so that others might comprehend or recognize hurtful and baseless opinions, for they do not move us any closer to a productive and normal life, let alone viable solutions. In fact, it is those words that often keep us from seeking help, as the stigma of others joined with the stigma in our own heads multiplies our struggle to come to terms with a life-altering and deeply isolating illness.

Our family may sound unique or atypical due to our level of loss and trauma, but we are certainly not special or rare. We are one family of millions. Our personal, painful, and unmistakable saga began over seventy years ago in another country, like so many families of that era.

Chapter One

Beginnings

My father was a kind and gentle man. Growing up with two brothers, his mother, his father, and many loving relatives in his extended family provided him with a wide circle of resources during his formative years. My father's parents originally came from Poland. They were devout Christians and wished, like all immigrants coming to America, to create a happy and successful life for their family in the land of opportunity, the United States of America.

They arrived on a cramped ship during a steady rain — the entire family as well as old neighbors, business associates, and family acquaintances. The inclement weather went unnoticed as they fulfilled a dream not only for themselves, but also for future generations.

They all settled in Brooklyn, New York, initially. Then a large portion of the family, including my father's parents, and some of their neighbors moved to Boston, while the others remained behind in Brooklyn.

My grandparents enrolled dad and his brothers in public school. They excelled academically, and seemed destined to become successful professionals and businessmen. They were smart, athletic, handsome, and popular, as well as kind and generous.

It was at this time that subtle signs of a transformation in my father's temperament were emerging, accompanied by others feeling that something wasn't right. It was unsettling, an obscure presence.

It was similar to a thunderstorm approaching from the distance. Though not yet visible to the eye, it brings a shift in the weather, the wind, and the sky. There is a tension in the air before actually seeing it. When the change finally occurs, it seems to happen in an instant, though many unnoticed things have already changed.

It was not clear to anyone what was happening to dad. They were unacquainted with the cunning nature of what *lies in silence*. The hidden storm crept into their presence — into dad's world — lurking and undetected. It was concealed, invisible, and nameless, as it has been throughout its existence.

Towards the end of dad's high school years, he experienced and exhibited an increase of frenetic energy — energy that was endless and often lacked direction or purpose. He swung between a "larger-than-life," jovial persona with a charismatic personality and a combative, unreasonable young man. Dad talked most often in a pressured manner, became involved in more activities than usual, perhaps more than was really possible, and, at times, demonstrated severe irritability and explosive anger.

The unfamiliar force was now fully interfering with every part of his life and all of his relationships. What remained undetected was now embarking on a mission to possess him.

At the start of his senior year most of his friends remained amused and entertained by his outgoing personality and his offbeat sense of humor, but they lacked any sense of who he was, as what they saw was not an authentic reflection of the illness quietly awakening beneath the surface.

By the end of dad's senior year, prior to graduation, most of his classmates feared him, as he had grown more unpredictable and had confusing outbursts not triggered by any specific event.

His lifestyle, which took years to establish, his academics, athletics, and social success all deteriorated. He was no longer welcome in those circles where he'd spent all of his childhood and adolescent years.

Dad was left isolated, lonely, and despondent. The timing of these unexplained life events could not have been worse. It caused him significant despair, and there were no explanations for his severe personality changes.

In an attempt to do something meaningful and honorable following high school, dad enlisted in the armed forces for four years. He served during a non-war era, and he felt proud contributing to the country that had provided so much opportunity for him and his family. But even this became a source of failure for him, as the original four years were cut to 18 months when he could not fulfill the required daily duties. Whatever he was struggling with followed him. His family was confused, and still no one understood the problem. Upon arriving home, dad started working full time, and shortly thereafter he met my mother.

My mother's family had also come to America about the same time as my father's. They hailed from Russia and England. They were strikingly different from my father's family, as his family was loud, opinionated, and were often melodramatic. Mom's family was perhaps not quite as intelligent, but what they lacked in IQ they made up for in grace, dignity, and character. Mom was a breath of fresh air, and conducted herself with quiet strength and elegance.

When my mother and father first met, it was a memorable meeting, as they immediately seemed to connect with one another on multiple levels. They liked the same music, the same activities, and they had similar goals. He didn't want to tell her at the beginning, but dad felt that mom was the woman he'd been hoping for years he would meet — his soul mate

He had a kind heart, a giving spirit, and goal-oriented dreams. Mom was a dark beauty and very popular with the boys. She liked dad's drive to succeed, as well as his handsome looks and kind-hearted spirit. She often referred to him as her "full package deal."

It brought a smile to his face and helped warm his young, weary, and heavy heart.

He began to feel loved and safe. Dad started having intimate feelings for mom, and it came at the right time, as he continued to feel abandoned by the only peer group he'd ever known in Boston. He was thankful that this kind-hearted and striking woman was helping him to heal his emotional scars, and he started looking forward to things getting more serious.

The chemistry between mom and dad led them to fall deeply in love. They each possessed an admirable sense of integrity and character, had extraordinary, sparkling dark brown eyes, and beautiful expressive faces, brightening every room they entered. They were the envy of many young people in the neighborhood, and quickly became popular and well liked in their circles. In addition to beauty, they also had a sense of loyalty and dedication to volunteer, and they spent many hours helping the community, the church, and others in need.

They enjoyed spending time together socializing, and they talked for hours into the night, whispering about their dreams and wishes for themselves and their future children.

On occasion dad took mom dancing, not something he enjoyed, but he knew it was one of mom's favorite activities in addition to music and singing. Mom knew he took her dancing in spite of his awkward moves and discomfort, so she returned the gesture by watching professional sporting events, though she could not tell the difference between a basketball and a football. They were a perfect couple in many ways.

They eventually set a date for their wedding, both feeling excited about new beginnings and their vision of a loving family.

Both sides of their families worked together to provide a modest ceremony for them at the local church. The minister was a kind, unassuming man, and genuinely liked both mom and dad. He was fondly known in the community as "hazel eyes." He had astonishing, breathtaking eyes that were deep pools of sparkling hazel. (In hushed tones, many talked of how distracting it was looking into his eyes, while in conversation about church matters.) He, as well as the community at large, immediately became part of my parent's extended family.

Family, friends, and congregants participated in the joyful celebration of friendship, love, and kinship that was the highlight and focus of their wedding day.

This was their day to mark a couple's love for one another. This was their day to commit to the future, "to love, honor, and cherish, in sickness and in health, through richer and poorer, until death do you part." Words that would be challenged in the future, in ways no one could imagine at the time.

Mom and dad's song then echoed through the church, played in a slow and lulling manner by the organist.

All of their invited guests watched as they mouthed the words to their song, staring at one another, as if no one else was present. Holding hands and gazing into each other's eyes, oblivious to the tearful happiness of the others sharing in their moment. The community bursting with hope, joy, and the ritual of shared beginnings. This was a family milestone and a lifecycle event.

This was their new beginning, their moment of intimacy underscored by their song, "More." The beginning lyrics described their feelings for each other in a way that all could understand as it marked the transformation of two separate individuals into one loving couple.

More than the greatest love the world has known,
This is the love I give to you alone.

It was a joyous day for everyone, as family and friends from all over came to celebrate the union of this beautiful, kind, and deserving couple.

However, as life has its ups and downs, it was not long before they were faced with their first difficult family event.

Soon after mom and dad married, dad's father passed away. He had been very sick with cancer and he'd suffered excruciatingly for an entire year. The onset of his cancer was acute, the treatments were painful, and his death came only weeks after their wedding. Grandmom slid into a deep depression over this period and isolated herself from the rest of the family. Following grandpop's death, her depression became worse, as a new normal fell upon her. She was now a widow.

Dad and his brothers mourned the loss of their father and discussed ways to care for their mother. Though grandmom was not old in years at 58 years old, she behaved like an elderly person in many ways. This added to their stress, as they all had young families and very busy lives. They agreed to share the responsibility for her daily welfare as much as possible, and look in on her regularly.

Mom and dad then proceeded to settle into a neat and tidy row house in a small town just outside of Boston. Life was taking shape for the two of them. Mom got pregnant, and they went on to have four children over the course of eight years. They were both gainfully employed with companies that paid well and offered generous benefits, which allowed them to enjoy a comfortable lifestyle.

They were a couple full of faith, attending church every Sunday, as well as an occasional special weekday service. Most times they dragged us along, and in the afternoon someone always cooked a large, traditional family meal. We were living the American dream and everything seemed to naturally fall into place. Life was fun, joyful, and meaningful on every level.

Dad followed all of the local teams with great enthusiasm. The Red Sox, Celtics, Bruins, and Patriots. His love of sports, his enthusiasm and support for the home teams, were all his way of being part of the city he now called home.

When he could afford it, he purchased two tickets to a sporting event, and we rotated attending games with him. On other game days we all sat in the living room watching our black and white console television and supporting our Boston and New England teams through all four seasons while enjoying the simple pleasures of quality family time.

When our teams played well enough to make the playoffs, we could count on delicious snacks and appetizers, as well as a crowd of cheerleaders sitting, standing, and pacing in our home, screaming and shouting as though one of us had hit the lottery.

We were very loud, fully dressed in team attire, and we critiqued each play, as though we knew better than the coaches and officials.

Dad was very animated during these times, and on occasion invited someone over from work or the neighborhood.

No different from other families in the area, we hollered and jumped up and down during the well-executed plays, and the not-so-well-executed ones. In addition, when there was a brilliant play, the high fives and high tens were part of the celebration. The moments are etched in my mind as priceless family memories.

There was a slow, predictable pace to our lives. We had our sports. We had family dinners together every night, unless there was a special church event or an extra-curricular school event. In addition to that, we often went to the drive-in movie theater located in town, and, though we did not have a large car, we still enjoyed movie after movie. The speaker was perfectly positioned on dad's driver-side door, and we proceeded to unload the snacks we had packed hours before. But popcorn was the treat for the evening. Fresh, hot, buttered popcorn.

Our favorite TV shows came on right after school and then again at night. My brother watched cartoons like "Speed Racer" and "Spiderman," while we typically watched "The Monkees" or the "Patty Duke Show." In the evening after we were each tucked into our small beds, we quietly made up games that were based on fantasies about princes and princesses. On occasion we would sneak out of our beds, crawl on our hands and knees, and hide at the top of the stairs, peering down into the living room. Usually there was a grown-up show on television, and at some point one of us would sneeze or whisper, giving ourselves away. Then we would all scamper back to our room. But our favorite family ritual, head and shoulders above the rest, was our weekly walk.

Sundays all of the kids walked to the corner store with just dad. We had him all to ourselves. This was our treasured time, as we developed silly rituals over the course of months. He allowed us to choose from among an assortment of items: chocolate covered pretzel rods, Pixie Stix, multi-colored dots stuck on long thin pieces of white paper, small wax bottles with sugary juice inside, or black and red shoestring licorice.

We all held hands crossing the street with our little fingers interlaced with one another. Dad was in the middle of our handholding line, and he would lightly jest with us about how we always picked the same dull item week after week. He called us predictable and boring. He worked hard to coax us into making an alternative choice in his playful manner, but we never did. He just chuckled, and we usually rolled our eyes while stifling our amusement. It was a regular game we all played week after week, and we never let on that we had any hint of the upcoming game or the outcome.

Dad's laugh was deep and genuine, and people within earshot often laughed as well. He had a contagious laugh in a resounding, soulful way. When dad laughed, we all joined him in a fit of giggles. These are my treasured family moments, most memorable and most missed. But what we did not know was that what *lies in silence* was on the horizon and about to steal my father away.

Our family, the school community, and the church community surrounded us with structure, strength, and predictability. Mom and dad were caring, hands-on parents, and though we did not have great wealth, we had something better. We had love, companionship, humor, spirituality, and a sense of safety in our world. A sense of safety that what *lies in silence* destroyed, along with all of us and everything our family had worked to achieve.

Chapter Two

Silent No More

Suddenly, out of the blue, chronic and severe sleeplessness took over dad's nights. He had problems falling asleep, and even when he got to sleep, he was not able to stay that way, often waking multiple times during the night. We often heard him pacing around in the wee hours of the morning.

He became agitated regularly and insignificant things often made him angry. He started having numerous problems at work, and he seemed to struggle on every level of his life, including minor family responsibilities.

No one knew what was happening to him. No one understood the drastic metamorphosis. Many dismissed it as normal stress or suppressed grief. Others made snap judgments and drew mistaken conclusions. All of these so-called answers could not have been further from the truth.

No one noticed the shrewd and fierce *silence* stirring. It was making plans for a grand entrance. Having the advantage of invisibility and soundlessness, no one recognized its ominous presence.

At that time, there was no real explanation or name for this emerging and drastic change. Family and friends were unable to fully grasp or understand what was to be the eventual shattering diagnosis, the so-called treatment, or the prognosis. Everyone had only theories: Perhaps the stress of military life had an effect on him? Perhaps having so many small children with those enormous responsibilities? Perhaps moving from Brooklyn to Boston? Perhaps grandpop's death?

Many family members, friends, colleagues, and professionals became involved. They all had theories; linear thinkers; cause and effect. A+B=C.

And as often happens in life, everyone had his or her own idea about what was going on. I remember overhearing daddy say (most likely when he was frustrated), "You know what they say about opinions? They're like assholes. Everybody has one."

One thing was certain. My father needed professional help and he needed it right away. I watched his eyes grow distant and vacant, and his soul slowly die and turn hollow. Without a whisper, a powerful force crept quietly into my daddy's brain and held him captive. It would no longer *lie in silence*, as the daddy I knew and loved with all my heart was gone.

While dad's medical condition deteriorated, the rest of us continued our daily life masquerading as a normal family. And to others we most likely appeared normal.

We attended school, took dance and piano lessons, played sports, went to recitals and school shows, played stickball and wall ball in the street with the neighborhood kids, enjoyed "The

Wonderful World of Disney," and watched "The Ed Sullivan Show" every week.

Nevertheless, we were far from a regular family. Our daily lives were filled with fear and confusion. We were scared, paralyzed, and overwhelmed. Our emotions were now intertwined with dad's mood, and how he felt set the tone for the moment. The chaos and unpredictability grew and redefined our existence. Still not one professional offered a reasonable explanation.

Therefore, when the answer finally came, it could not have been more devastating. Stigma, ineffective treatment, and a world with little knowledge or tolerance were to be our future. The diagnosis was life altering for dad and for the rest of the family.

We were told dad had a serious, pervasive, and debilitating mental illness — an illness surging like an out-of-control, violent, and uncontainable geyser. He was similar to a volcano where the only safe option was to watch from a distance, because the intensity placed your safety at great risk. Unfortunately we didn't have the option of distance. Dad's flashing moments of rage came more and more frequently. He was disordered in his thinking, grandiose, and hostile most days. I was sad and frightened often, crying as I watched my mentally healthy father, who was pleasant and even-keeled, kind and sensitive, loving and caring transform into someone I didn't know, and I struggled to love.

As I look at this in 2009, it is clear to me that I lost my father and a large chunk of my childhood to bipolar disorder. A disease that continues to take those that I love most, while creating catastrophic losses I still cannot grasp.

HIGHLY GENETIC!

I watch in horror with a heavy ache in my heart, while multiple generations of my family and other families struggle to live with this mental illness in a world with inadequate treatment, a disintegrating mental health care system, and stigma that wounds the souls of everyone associated with the disease to the very core. The same bipolar disease passed on to my children and me.

Bipolar, like many other diseases, does not distinguish between cultures. No race, creed, religion, gender, sexual orientation, age, level of education, or socioeconomic status prevents its debilitating and aggressive onset.

It does not differentiate between homelessness, home ownership, sobriety, addictions of any kind, those on disability income, those who are wealthy, and those who enjoy freedom or those who are incarcerated. Bipolar does not care if you are a physician, a teacher, a lawyer, a janitor, a politician, a celebrity, a carpenter, a fast food worker, a toddler, or a middle school student.

HIGHLY GENETIC!

Bipolar disorder is one of the most heritable mental illnesses based on my personal experience, the experience of others in my circle, and my observations through my profession.

The disorder has now abducted more than ten of my family members. I lost what once was a family with a future and now have only a future that was.

This is our family's natural disaster; bipolar is our tsunami. The beginning of our mass drowning in a mental illness, taking more hostages with each generation — one heaving, violent, and fatal wave at a time.

HIGHLY GENETIC!

I do not mean to imply that all people who suffer from mental illness are violent. In addition, I recognize there are many high functioning, mood-disordered people living fairly normal lives between episodes and with mild symptoms that break through along the way.

However, in my opinion it is a disservice and miscalculation to separate mental illness from other long-term, chronic sociological issues. Every area of our culture appears to be showing an increase in violence, such as violent lyrics in some types of music, suicide by firearms, and the devastating emergence of school shootings. We have become more sexualized, as television shows no longer seem to have adult time slots, and many adolescents choose provocative clothing that mimics pop culture, particularly *those who target that audience. Addictions are increasing, age of addiction is getting lower, and we are addicted in more ways. Both substance and process addictions are getting worse, as we can see from substance dependence, sexual addiction becoming a major industry, food addiction, and shopping addiction. The interaction between mental illness and our current culture provides an accessible and lethal co-existence that makes both worse.*

HIGHLY GENETIC!

As a young child I thought I'd lost my childhood to a father with anger issues. For decades, I misinterpreted these violent rages as childhood physical abuse. It is crystal clear to me now that the rages were a symptom of dad's illness: bipolar disorder, an insidious, life-altering disease of the brain.

Dad could no longer regulate any emotion. His brain did not allow that function any longer. His anger triggered him to violently hurl our family dog down the steps, as though heaving a boulder into a quarry. He threw chairs across our kitchen, ripped the heads off our Barbie dolls, and, on more occasions than I care to remember, turned his anger on me. He and I both became regular victims of his bipolar disorder.

The disease was running our family now. Make no mistake about it; the illness was in charge. What had been *lying in silence* was present and consuming the kind man who once was my father.

We watched in horror as the dad we loved disintegrated before our very eyes. What had emerged was becoming an uninvited member of our family. Moreover, its intention was to extinguish everyone I loved, one generation at a time.

No class for anger management could improve this situation, even if there had been a class. This was not a condition helped by finding his inner child, resolving old grief, psychoanalysis, revealing his authentic self for a richer life, coming over from the dark side, or finding the seat of his soul. An epileptic cannot will himself or herself not to have a seizure. Those who suffer with a tic disorder cannot stop their painful tics and unwelcome movements or vocalizations.

Bipolar is neurobiological. It is a disease of the brain. Medical treatment is necessary.

Sadly the medical treatment was not yet available. This was beyond what my father or my family or even the doctors we saw could handle. It is hard to grasp as an adult. When I was a child, I felt only terror looking to my daddy and finding a powerful, unwanted, and destructive tyrant instead of a safe, warm, and gentle guide.

Then, after a couple years of raging followed by horrible regret for his actions, the delusions came to the front door of dad's brain.

They did not knock nor ring the bell. Psychosis forcefully burst in.

The exhausting chase began. Running after and running from a silent and invisible menacing stalker.

Though dad had started medication and counseling, as is often the case with severe mental illness, the symptoms never stayed away for long. They would come and go, creating an unpredictable emotional ride, not healthy for any young family.

And as symptoms subsided and quieted down some, we knew it was merely a pause, only an illusion of safety. Similar to a high-level member of a terrorist cell or an individual in a large drug-dealing organization, one symptom would go, but another one would quickly step in to take its place.

Our lives changed drastically. We could no longer afford dance instruction nor piano lessons.

Professional sporting events were now too expensive and all activities that cost money were eliminated. We no longer took walks to the corner store and most of the family and friends in our circle stopped calling and visiting. The long journey of fear, loneliness, and isolation began. And so did the endless list of grief and loss.

The judgment on mom and dad was extremely hurtful, and we experienced horrendous stigma from inside as well as outside our family unit. People who identified themselves as good Christians quickly demonstrated the definition of hypocrisy, often spreading gossip and rumors that were repeated by their children. People say that kids are cruel, but I have learned adults are worse.

Mom applied for food stamps, which clearly had an emotional effect on her, as I caught her crying on the edge of her bed after the welfare appointment.

We stopped going out as much in public, and our home became akin to a terrorists' cave.

The radical extremist cell was now living in my father's brain. I no longer knew who he was, as the illness permanently moved into his psyche.

We watched with deep sadness as he lost his brilliant mind, his physically fit body, his caring spirit, his sensitive heart, and his kind soul. Gone. Lost. Vanished without a trace.

When I dared to look into dad's eyes, I now saw rage, delusion, and a deep, bottomless grief. His beautiful brown eyes with lashes like sweepers looked blank and vacant. The father I once knew and loved disappeared. His joy was devoured. So were his humor and his spirit, his life and his soul, his dignity and his pride. All erased with one disease. That which *lies in silence* swallowed my dad. It was emotionally crushing for him and all of us who loved him. One disease obliterating my entire family's existence.

Once we were a spontaneous family and inspired by many things. If something went wrong, we had the chance to erase the hurt and start over. No longer. Starting over was not an option.

Like a broken Etch-a-Sketch, the lever slid to the right. Everything was upside down. The disappearance of our family drawing commenced.

Chapter Three

Has Anybody Seen My Daddy?

Somewhere around my tenth birthday dad started spiraling down into a permanent abyss where no medicine, no professionals, no clergy, no family members, and no friends could reach him. He lost job after job and we depended on the help of others for the first time ever.

Money was always tight and we lived in a chronic state of anxiety. Dad was home more often, and his actions became more dangerous, violent, and unpredictable.

At one point, he was hospitalized for a couple of months and continued to receive mental health services after that, but nothing ever seemed to last. He'd have a positive response to some new medication that brought a flickering hopeful moment of seeing the real man inside the illness. Within days or weeks, though, he could no longer manage the noise in his head. The disease would shatter his stability and wreak havoc once again on our daily routine. His brain became activated, which caused him great emotional pain. The symptoms would abduct everything in him that was decent and healthy.

Dad seemed slightly aware something was happening to him. He looked frightened and defeated. Terrified. We watched painfully as his racing thoughts and delusions held him hostage. It was gut wrenching to witness and we were helpless to make him better.

He was a walking time bomb as the wires in his brain crossed, causing overproduction and underproduction of vital neural transmitters necessary to function. His illness damaged the wiring in his brain responsible for the most vital pieces of being human: physical functioning, mental clarity, normal range of emotions, and the ability to experience one's own spirituality.

It was only a matter of time before the electrical system sparked, starting a massive disconnect from normal thoughts and moving it further into insanity.

This is the series of events that cause destruction and fear for many families suffering with mental illness.

We lived in a state of uneasiness every day. This was in our own home and in our own community. Places that used to be safe, warm, familiar, and comforting were that way no longer. There was nowhere to hide and nothing felt safe.

Dad's delusions took over his thought processes and became his reality. The pictures created in his mind by his illness were not what the rest of us saw. His cognitive "movie" didn't match the rest of the world any more.

He became fixated on politics, religion, newspaper reporters, celebrity anchors, and high-level religious leaders.

He obsessed about finding someone to hold accountable, someone to pay for the loss of his family, the loss of his career, the loss of his dignity, and the loss of his life.

Dad felt emasculated. He felt betrayed and deceived. He was impotent to change his situation. He struggled with the concept of having all this opportunity in America, such as buying a home, marrying his true love, having a family and a career where he flourished, only to now lose it all to an illness in his brain that had no cure, no reasonable treatment, and offered no hope of long-term stability.

A small part of him was aware. He felt deep sorrow, as did the rest of us. He cried and violently raged for hours at a time. There was no consoling him, and we could only watch in horror as he grew even more unstable.

As dad grew sicker, mom could no longer keep us safe, so we moved in with another family member. Dad's behavior was always unpredictable, and the danger now outweighed the balance of love and joy that once was there.

We packed all of our belongings, placed everything we needed into our old Chevy, and abandoned my dad in order to have safety. We left him while he was sick, dangerous, and lost.

It was an overwhelming moment.

It didn't seem right.

Why would we leave daddy when he is sick?

This was a decision born out of desperation, a decision no one should ever have to make, a decision that is made by thousands every day. Today was our day.

None of us spoke while riding in the car, as we all dealt with our own suffering, our own pain, our own loss, and our own grief. The disease was winning. Yet, there was more to come. The future held things we could never have prepared for, and what *lies in silence* held tragedy and heartbreak that remains immeasurable, inconceivable, and mercilessly incomprehensible.

For the next couple of years we lived a life where we pretended to survive and even excel. With the physical separation from my father, we achieved some psychological distance from the illness. Less daily chaos, I suppose.

Out of sight, out of mind, a trick we all play in our lives. A game and a coping strategy that allows the mind, the heart, and the human spirit to rest — until the next round of trauma arrives.

Dad's grief from his loss of self, loss of his marriage, and the loss of his children became another source of obsession. He often called and hung up, listening quietly to the soft voice of whoever answered the phone. He desperately yearned for the old life we'd had, and the children and wife he once provided for and cared for. Dad was despondent and he spent many hours in agony and mental torture, as he could not manage the emotions of grief caused by our move. He missed us as much as or more than we all missed him. We were missing him before we moved. He'd been gone long before then.

Dad sometimes watched us for hours, usually from a distance. He sat outside of our house, outside of our school, and, on occasion, we caught a glimpse of him outside while we played stickball, wall ball, and freeze tag. It terrified my mother.

We didn't understand what was happening. It was confusing and sad. It was stressful and difficult. We were very young. We missed our healthy daddy. Who was this scary man who merely lurked outside our lives when he used to nurture our hearts and our spirits? This was not our father.

Fatherhood had always been a fulfilling role in dad's life and an integral part of his character. It was a joyful responsibility for him and a significant portion of his identity before mental illness.

We all mourned for our life before bipolar, much like a family mourns for lost life after a major car accident that leaves traumatic brain injury in its wake; or when someone is suffering after having a life-altering stroke. There are many illnesses where there seems to be a starting line, but the journey to the end of all of them can be long and unpredictable. Nothing is ever the same as it was before. Nothing is the same from one day to the next. Nothing.

The end looms ominously in the future. Daily hardship can be exhausting and hopeless. In the movie *Groundhog Day* the hero awoke to the same day over and over, but his task was to "get it right." With severe and chronic bipolar you wake to a day of exhaustion and suffering. "Getting it right" isn't an option.

Getting through the day IS the goal. Every day.

Chapter Four

He Lies In Silence

Several years later while watching "I Love Lucy," a daily after school ritual, I heard the telephone ring. Not a normal type of ring, but a constant, persistent every couple of minutes ringing. A family member yelled from upstairs not to pick up the telephone. It was a loud, no-nonsense yell.

As a twelve year old, that merely increased my curiosity. I listened in on the next call and heard *"Boston Globe"* and "We have no comment."

Not allowed to answer the phone?

What did "no comment" mean?

I felt a tight, sickening knot in my stomach and I didn't yet know why.

It was at that moment the phone was removed from its cradle. I heard the loud buzzing sound indicating someone had purposely interrupted our phone service. My curiosity turned into worry. Intense worry.

I found out later that the severity of my anxiety and the depth of my concern were intuitive. My premonition of pending doom was painfully on target. Our lives were about to change forever, yet again, and it was going to be more devastating and shamefully public.

The rest of my siblings came home from school an hour later. My mother sat us down side by side on the long, turquoise sofa with plastic slipcovers in the living room. Several other family members were also present. They all looked traumatized and very nervous.

Mom proceeded to tell us a story that I was not fully able to grasp at the time. It was more than my twelve-year-old brain could understand.

It was the first of many incomprehensible tragedies in my life. Tragedies caused by bipolar disorder: a voracious, ravenous, unquenchable disease of the brain that causes pain and sorrow in the blink of an eye; a genetic monster.

She spoke slowly, just above a whisper. "Something horrible happened today. I need to tell you something really difficult and upsetting. If you want to cry or listen to only a part of it, that's fine. All of the family members here have offered their support for all of us. The same few people who have been there for us all along. They're here now."

Mom started to wring her hands nervously, something she did only during the most stressful of times. I tried to brace myself, but there is nothing that prepares you for this type of situation.

"Your dad was involved in a very tragic situation today. I don't have any answers, but I need to tell you what happened. Okay?"

We all nodded slowly with great trepidation. I was thinking we'd already been through hell. How much worse could it get?

"The police have told us that daddy built a bomb and somehow got ahold of some weapons, mostly guns, and then he went to our church."

Mom paused, wiping tears as they streamed down her face. She looked ashen and exhausted, and she took a deep breath so that she could continue.

"Daddy then forced his way into a private area of our church. He grabbed our minister and held him hostage."

Mom dabbed at her eyes as the tears were coming faster and faster. Rather than drops of tears, there was now an uncontrollable flow of waves coming from her eyes, stemming from the deep, mounting sorrow she felt.

She continued in a coarse whisper, while someone moved behind her, resting their hands on her shoulders, as though willing her the strength to continue. A simple gesture of support that I interpreted as imminent disaster.

"Your dad then demanded to know why he was sick. He demanded to know why we left him. He demanded to know why there was no cure for bipolar."

Dad demanded our minister telephone someone of higher authority in the church. He threatened to blow up the church with the homemade bomb, and said he'd kill anyone who survived by his own hand.

Fearing for his life, the minister called an associate of his from the neighboring church.

He explained cryptically what was going on. While the minister was on the phone, dad got increasingly agitated. He started pacing back and forth and his paranoia surged. He shouted for him to hang up the telephone while shoving one of the loaded guns into his side.

NOW I WANT YOU TO CALL GOD!!!

CALL GOD, MR. HAZEL EYES!!!

CALL GOD NOW!!!

DO IT!!!

I WANT ANSWERS!!!

WHY AM I SUFFERING LIKE THIS?

Dad began to sob. A deep, heavy, and uncontrollable sobbing. His face was flushed a deep shade of red and tear-stained, and he broke out into a cold, clammy sweat.

He then dropped to one knee.

While crying and struggling with his thoughts, dad turned to the minister and whispered quietly…

Why are my children afraid of me?

Why can't I keep a job and provide for them?

Why did the woman I love leave me?

The minister attempted to offer counsel, believing there was a shift in dad's demeanor. He was relying on the years they worked together in the community. He was unfamiliar with the severity of dad's illness and had not seen him in quite some time.

At that moment, he realized he had not visited dad or our family though he had heard countless rumors that we were struggling. He experienced a moment of guilt and then quickly composed himself, hoping to break through the clutches of dad's instability.

Looking back as an adult, I can see why our minister attempted to reason with my dad, but he was doomed to fail. The reasoning section of dad's brain was damaged. Much of his executive function was damaged and my dad had very little reasoning capability. Neurologically, the majority of his mind in charge of reasoning and critical thinking did not exist. He lost much of it when he got sick, and medication only brought so much back. Our minister was completely unaware of the strength and deceptive nature of his opponent.

Dad continued to sob and gasp for air. He had reached his breaking point and was looking for answers. He was looking for guidance. He was looking for reason. He was looking for explanations and simplicity in a circumstance that had no solutions then and still has few solutions now.

After a minute of deafening silence, he started screaming again at the top of his lungs.

"I WANT AN ANSWER, DAMMIT, AND I WANT IT NOW!!!"

Dad was getting more restless and impatient. He raised his head and stood upright. He was not aware that the police and other armed forces were surrounding the church. The neighboring minister had placed a call to 911. Snipers had taken up positions all around the cathedral, our family's house of worship. The scene then took a drastic turn for the worse.

Dad's brain disorder fully took over and he started shooting randomly. His random shots connected with many parishioners praying in the sanctuary.

He was in a painful, mixed manic state, and lost all impulse control and rational thought — two indicators of his type of bipolar disorder. Psychosis led the way and took full command, overpowering both dad and the minister. Dad's brain and body were the vehicle of his illness and a victim of his own brain chemistry. He took several hostages.

Some of the church members who had been praying were now lying on the floor. They were covered in blood and crying as quietly as possible, for fear of calling attention to themselves. The stream of bullets hit many of them.

The storm of mental illness fiercely burned within dad's mind, dad's body, dad's soul, and dad's spirit. The darkness and dad fully merged. As dad slowly turned toward our minister, the core of the disease was in control.

Dad and the disease, now one, leaned over and stared into the gentle, hazel eyes of our minister. He continued to cry while pushing the dark illness back a bit in order to have his voice and message heard one last time.

He addressed the minister in a hushed tone. "It is your fault I am sick. I have come here and prayed with my family. I have donated money and hours of time to your church, and I have helped those who are deprived in our community. I served in the military and I have always helped others in need. And yet, I am sick. I have bipolar disorder. I suffer every day. Moreover, no one cares. Not even you."

He continued to speak quietly in a fixed and drone-like manner while he fought the internal battle for domination. He stumbled on. "Minister, people avoid me. I hurt my children and my wife. I see bloody violent movies in my head, and no matter how much medicine I take, they won't go away. I am mocked, stigmatized, and alone. I am incompetent in every task I attempt. I feel valueless and worthless. People treat me like a leper, not with love and compassion as before. You taught me that God and faith heal all, yet you haven't brought that healing to me. You tell *lies in silence* just like the doctors. Hell is not in the afterlife, preacher man. Hell lives in my head and is now my life."

Dad paused as if he was contemplating surrender, but the other voice in his head whispered/screamed a different plan. Dad could no longer restrain what *lies in silence*. He had done what he could to find words for his feelings and he could no longer hold back his impulses. The bloody images he always saw became his reality.

In one motion the illness/dad raised his arm. Boom. Boom. Boom. From one of his guns he fired three bullets into the face of our beloved, helpless minister.

The man who married dad and mom. The man who shared and guided our lives for so many years. The beautiful soft face that held those magnificent hazel eyes.

The scene was like a war zone with bipolar disorder continuing to hold its claim, creating horror and destruction of enormous proportion.

Now masquerading as my father, the dark and violent symptoms of psychosis, one of the trademarks for some of those with mental illness, took aim and shot directly into the face of our minister while horrified parishioners looked on with panic. The gaping wound made him unrecognizable, and others knew at that very moment that the minister would forever *lie in silence*. He was dead. The disease successfully transformed dad by his own hand into a murderer.

Dozens of loud blasts then sounded as police fired a hailstorm of bullets into the sanctuary, many hitting dad as he stood staring down at our minister.

And though he seemed to know that in an instant he was finally going to have peace in his brain, he sped up the process. Dad surrendered to his illness, unable and unwilling to fight any longer.

What remains unclear is whether my stable dad himself or the unstable illness that hijacked my dad initiated what happened next. He bent his arm, slowly raising one of the guns that he still held in his hand, took precise aim, and fired. Bipolar disorder, my father, or both of them shot my daddy in the head. The illness and my father now *lie in silence*. They were both dead. A victory for no one.

My father had been delusional, agitated, and completely lost in an abyss. An abyss of what used to be the beautiful father who walked us to the corner store every Sunday. It was not about the candy. It was about the moment in time. It was gone.

Gone with him were all of the good memories and all of the bad. Gone were the mystery, the uncertainty, and the crater of emotions, often the greeting card sent by mental illness. Not for a holiday. Not for a celebration. Simply a daily memo of heartbreak and misfortune.

The danger and chaos were now permanently quiet. Silenced by dad's own hand.

His mental battle could no longer bring suffering to him or the ones he loved. He killed the terrorist gene passed down from generations before. He took control the only way it seemed possible. He eliminated his suffering and pain.

No one would ever know if his suicide was the result of dad's internal delusions and psychosis, or the result of a voluntary and spontaneous decision: a decision to sacrifice his own life. No one would ever know if he fully comprehended that the now materialized mental illness had no bounds or limits in its unquenchable desire to inflict suffering and desolation.

All I knew was that my daddy was dead. The dad who let me ride horsy on his back. The dad who read bedtime stories to us every night. The dad who tightly held my hand to cross the street while joking on the way to the corner store.

My dad, my memories, my safety, and my childhood were erased like chalk from a chalkboard. My innocence was taken, and I was about to learn the other harsh realities and lessons of the burden of living in any family with mental illness, and especially those with multi-generational mental illness.

With the vengeance and randomness of a tornado, the destruction upon us was broadening.

The forecast was that more devastating storms were to follow. My family lacked any of the items necessary for extreme weather conditions, and the few items we had would never keep us safe in the ensuing torrent of mental illness. There was no safe place to go and hide.

I was unsure of everything in my life. Time stood still. I gulped for air feeling dizzy and faint.

My mother stopped speaking at that moment. It had taken a lot out of her to tell us the entire story, a task that had to be thorough because the media were rushing to put their sensational and damning spin on it. There was already a large group of reporters at the door, and it was all too surreal to grasp. We faced the loss of dad and the violation of our privacy all happening within minutes of each other.

We were suddenly under a microscope as strangers and outsiders took turns looking through the eyepiece. Our most personal and painful moments were about to be judged by the general public, most of whom had no sympathy or understanding about mental illness as it really is. We braced ourselves for the deluge of unwelcome, hurtful, and unjustified criticism.

The deluge came. It came over and over again. We quickly learned nothing exists to prepare for a monsoon of stigma and judgment, in addition to the lack of privacy and complete disrespect to such personal pain and tragedy.

No one is ever ready for something like this. No one.

Chapter Five

Incomprehensible Childhood Lessons

Since my family refused all interviews, it was inevitable that the media would write and report inaccurate information, and discredit as well as dishonor dad's reputation. He would be portrayed as an evil and cold-blooded killer.

The evening news was reported the same way as usual, except this night my father was the top story.

Newspaper reporters and television reporters swarmed around our house, our front door, and our neighborhood. They were like rodents fighting over scraps of waste in a dumpster, hunting for "the kill" and the "truth" behind the violence.

Mom had to tell us everything. Her fear was that sleazy reporters would stalk us at school and in the community. Mom was right. They did. Some of us were in elementary school.

They approached our friends and the parents of our friends outside our schoolyard. Their questions were about my father's character and if he had any history of violence. They pursued and chased until someone answered what they demanded to know.

Why did this happen?

My friends and I were frightened much of the time and cried often while the story remained prominent in the news. We did not understand how one day we used Crayola crayons, played tag in the yard, and compared notes on whose birthday party was next, while the next day we were crushed by a media frenzy and the enormous tragedy of a public murder-suicide.

We were bombarded by adult reporters, asking us about homicide and suicide. Teachers, administrators, and parents did their best to provide some level of protection, but they were outnumbered.

We felt contaminated as what was once a quiet, safe elementary school turned into a large tank where sharks and poisonous sea creatures worked as teams to chase, overpower, and devour our little school of guppies.

None of them reported it accurately. Not one. It appeared as though they focused solely on their own addiction to sensationalize and never once considered the real and tragic story that was behind dad's actions.

What they reported was incorrect and mistaken, and it was a disservice to my entire family, as well as to the public at large. As a young girl I learned early how people sell their ethics, their integrity, their moral fiber, their character, and their credibility for the wrong story. It made no sense. They asked in multiple articles: Was his marriage on the rocks? Was he a chronically unemployed freeloader? Did he have a conflict with the church or the minister? Was he broke and unable to pay the bills? All the questions assumed a normalcy that simply wasn't there.

The reporters in those days were misguided and deceived by their own perceptions of what was possible. The majority remained smug, condescending, and unbelievably arrogant in their assumptions and finger pointing at a man and a family they knew nothing about. They all speculated about a motive.

What was this man's motive?

Motive? He was mentally ill.

Motive? He suffered from bipolar disorder.

Mental disorders need no motive. What lies in silence *can be indiscriminate and random. Reporters failed to recognize or use words pertaining to mental illness, failed treatment, inadequate medications, family suffering, genetics, or life-altering disease. Not one. They all wrote sensational stories of murder and suicide.*

Motive? A question as absurd as looking for a motive for an epileptic seizure.

Motive? A question as absurd as having a motive for a diabetic coma.

Motive? A question as absurd as a motive for muscle twitching and visual disturbance in multiple sclerosis.

They were absurd. They were uneducated, ill-advised, and mistaken. It was at that point in my life that I learned to doubt adults in general. They taught me by their own actions. What became clear was that most in the media were ignorant about the intricacies and clinical complications of mental illness. They searched for situational (and sensational) answers when the answer often was simply mental illness. They rushed to judge, stigmatize, and humiliate families already suffering years of pain and fear, often reporting information served with an egotistical air of condescension.

There have been some minor improvements in this realm, but the issue of motive continues to be the first line of questioning. Talk shows seem driven by others' tragedy, the lack of clinical understanding provides a larger platform for judgment and stigma, and the media in general focus on sensational details rather than the complexity clearly related to severe mental health disorders. On occasion there are stories about mental illness in more accurate and sometimes compassionate terms, but there is still a very long way to go before the media, medical establishment, and general public really grasp the depth of suffering that results from bipolar disorder, the mood disorder spectrum, and severe and chronic mental illness.

Our church community was also horribly traumatized. Countless numbers of families were affected. My father had never hurt another human being while healthy and well. Nevertheless, his sick brain triggered him to act in ways that were not human. Not compassionate. Not loving, kind, or thoughtful. This was not my father. This was the mark left by severe, chronic, and persistent mental illness.

The church community did not understand bipolar disorder and they were not forgiving either. The loss and shame were too overwhelming for them to handle. The loss column was adding up, and we were all too grief-stricken and suffering post-traumatic stress symptoms for any effective treatment.

I tried to come to grips with dad's suicide and, perhaps more hauntingly, the victims of his homicide. In total, five people were dead. Three church members, the minister, and my father. I soon figured out that coming to grips is merely a phrase. No grips came.

I felt sick to my stomach all the time. I felt helpless and ashamed. If my minister could not help and dad's doctors could not help, what did that mean?

Was there no hope?

Could anyone or anything help?

The funeral and the burial were held some time later. The casket was closed and there was no viewing. This was decided early on due to the condition of my father's body, his face, his head, and his skull. My grandmother threw herself across his coffin, and dad's siblings had to pry her fingers away one by one, so they could move the casket down the aisle. It was a vividly agonizing scene, as she was being forced to physically let go of her son, a task she had already tried to do emotionally while he sank further into his illness.

As a child, this was one of the scenes that made a permanent imprint on the corridors of my impressionable mind. The same young corridors that were quickly getting longer and more crowded. Perhaps my most devastating memory was immediately following the service, when my mother, without any warning, dramatically collapsed to the floor.

I watched in horror as her knees buckled and she crumbled to the ground while others raced to catch her. She was overcome with the pain of losing dad to his disease while at the same time feeling some relief of the daily terror ending. So she thought.

Mom and dad had shared a loving marriage for a long time before bipolar took him hostage. She lost her best friend, her life partner, and the father of their children. It was a shocking, unrecoverable loss. My heart ached for her and for us.

Chapter Six

The Infinite Gift of Stigma

After a long period of mourning, we returned to school. The staring, whispering, ridiculing, and name-calling were hurtful and overwhelming. This was to be the next step in the journey of chronic loss, stigma, and isolation.

We were shunned to some degree or another, and we found that religious people can be just as judgmental as those who do not believe in a higher power. Perhaps worse, as they shout things about the devil, hell, sinning, retribution, and revenge.

My faith and my spirituality both in and out of my community began to waiver. We became more isolated because of mental illness. Others viewed us as freaks. They had read the newspaper version of the incident. They didn't get it. They weren't interested in getting it. They were afraid to ask questions; we were afraid to offer any explanation due to intolerance and stigma; and so most others were left to believe the slanted media version of the atrocity. Unfair. Unjust. I define it as media victimization. An added dimension of a family's personal and catastrophic new normal.

Eventually we were forced to change schools and change churches. It was excruciating as the level of our emotional exhaustion kept rising. Another loss for the list. They were mounting. My heart and my stomach hurt daily and I started having migraine headaches.

For months, there were articles in the newspaper. Dad was described in the most stigmatizing, uneducated, insensitive, and irresponsible ways. Crazy, foolish, evil, whacko, nuts, lazy, bum, failure, psycho, fanatic, atheist, and pathetic. No one seemed to understand mental illness. None of the articles were sensitive to the traumatized survivors.

Writers often used some of the most offensive, degrading, negative comments. I wonder if they would also have written about Alzheimer's, brain cancer, head trauma, or any other brain disease in such a de-humanizing manner. I wonder how reporters would tell the same story now.

Part of our new normal routine was going to individual and family counseling. Sometimes the kids spoke to the psychologist alone and sometimes we went in as a whole family. Most of the time, I was quiet because I didn't know what to talk about.

Where would I begin in my journey of loss and grief in a sixty-minute session?

In addition to that, I was not aware that mom and our psychologist were tracking and observing my sisters and brother, because some of them were showing signs of early onset (pediatric) bipolar disorder.

I sat silently. I felt nothing but distrust for grown-ups, since I believed they told *lies in silence*. I didn't understand that my father lost his battle with bipolar and that was the only reason we lost him. In fact, we'd lost him long before he took his own life and the lives of others.

And now something unthinkable and horribly possible: the next generation was getting sick. It was too hard to understand. It took my mother's breath away.

Her spirit and her soul seemed irreparably damaged as she mourned the loss of her husband, and now, only months later, she sought evaluations for some of her children. Evaluations that could show signs of more family members slain by mood disorders setting its sights on destroying the next generation.

It was inconceivable. There was no way to prevent the genetics from moving on. We were helpless, vulnerable, and powerless again. We waited and watched. Mental illness crept back the same way as before. Invisible and silent.

Months later one of my older sisters developed further signs of unstable mood. This came after successfully completing high school. Mom spent a lot of time seeking help for her mental health to no avail.

She began cutting herself on a regular basis, using anything she could find, to create the surge of chemicals that somehow helped her to cope for the moment. Mom started to lock up anything she could, including razor blades, safety pins, knives, nail clippers, and paper clips.

In addition to self-injury, she began bingeing and purging, developing severe symptoms of bulimia. All of these were danger signs that she may have an emerging mental disorder, as what *lies in silence* began to swallow another one of our family members. Like a snake, first wrapping itself around a rodent, to strangle and suffocate it until it can swallow the lifeless body, dead and whole. In the end, the illness won again.

At the age of eighteen, my sister disappeared, moving halfway across the country to be with a man getting out of prison, a stranger she had been secretly corresponding with.

And as if my mother and my family had not suffered enough, my brother began abusing alcohol and drugs, acting out in many ways that identified him as likely having an early onset mood disorder.

Their lives were marked by hypersexuality (excessive and provocative sex acts or sexual behaviors), as well as an inability to maintain employment, irrational and impulsive decision-making, and anger that came and went in a flash on a regular basis. Anger not obviously triggered by an event. Sleep had also always been a problem for some of my siblings, but no one connected the dots. That is until now.

My father's actions and the aftermath led to severe post-traumatic stress disorder (a term not even used when this all happened). The PTSD and the genetics created a deadly combination, hard to diagnose and even harder to understand. The seed of mental illness took root, and in an instant claimed the next generation.

My mother slipped into a dark depression, something she had struggled with for years, but this was the darkest and deepest by far. She was emotionally preparing to bury all four of her children. And still not one professional mentioned the words genetic, inherited, highly heritable illness. Not one. They told *lies in silence*.

I had more questions.

Why the deafening *lies in silence*?

Wasn't there enough evidence to warn families?

Are three generations enough to claim this as genetic?

Four generations? Five generations of suffering? Was there a magic number?

Why the disconcerting lack of urgency?

Why the absence of strong voices from the mental health and medical communities shouting about genetics?

Why no warnings or precautions for families with these genetics so that this did not become a horrible legacy to millions?

Why no loud public discussions as the suicide rate increased?

Why no loud national outcry?

The answers wouldn't come until much later. And by then, it was too late. Much too late. We were losing each battle and the medical community remained quiet about the high probability that this was a genetic illness. Neurobiological in nature. Permanent cognitive effects. A younger age of onset than previously believed, often with severe co-occurring disorders, and with more extreme suffering and painful, life-altering symptoms.

Where were the clinical and scientific voices of guidance?

Were we lying in silence based on fear, based on hurt, based on shame?

If only we had had the Depression Bipolar Support Alliance (DBSA) and the National Institute of Mental Health (NIMH), but they were not speaking out on these issues yet. The alarms sounded by those organizations came later. At the time it was a deafening silence.

They did not look at families already suffering. Hemingway and Hartley as well as many others. Multiple diagnoses. Multiple suicides. A mental illness that is highly genetic with a significant risk of multiple tragedies.

I feel most betrayed by these lies in silence. No one spoke. No one sounded the bells. No one warned the families. Not one professional. Not one. It is something I have never forgotten. While growing up I did not understand that this was a profession struggling to find answers as well, often with inadequate or linear training and lack of scientific information. And though there were a few who suspected, based on clear generational links, without research to back them up they remained quiet.

As I grew and matured, the events in my childhood stayed with me. Though therapists told me the pain would diminish over time with counseling I can assure you the opposite is true.

As I became an adult and I understood more, the grief and trauma grew with me.

I was not immobilized, but I had a very clear sense the darkness was still here, merely lying quietly. Waiting. I shuddered to think my premonition could be correct.

Over the years, dad's story was repeated in church gatherings, conferences for religious leaders, and was often used in training police forces. On occasion, it was referred to on a talk show and, any time a similar shooting occurred, it was back in the headlines.

Dad's name, his victim's names, and all of the painful memories dug up along with all of the grief.

It became an unmanageable wound — a wound where someone else keeps ripping off the scab to destroy whatever healing may have occurred, leaving me with even deeper scars.

At one point, a Hollywood actor mentioned my dad while he was crusading and proselytizing about the myth of mental illness. His opinion was that mental illness did not exist. He served up an incredible portion of grandiosity, accompanied by a large slice of ignorance and a ladle full of disrespect. Having no platform but intolerance, he tried to discredit the reality lived by millions of people.

It was as if somehow celebrity made him an expert on mental illness and the suffering of families. His beliefs were religious rather than informed. Yet, he continued his tirade as though he was a messiah of neurobiology.

My family felt victimized and voiceless again because of those preaching false sermons with no personal experience. It added to our feelings of ridicule and uninformed criticism

This, by far, continued to be the worst form of stigma — an outsider denying and invalidating our life journey. This was an uninvited visitor in our home, challenging our perception of our own life: who we are, what we have learned, and how we see the world. Celebrity victimization. Media victimization. Over and over. A type of abuse that goes without punishment or consequence — protected by free speech. Difficult lessons to learn. I was tired of lessons.

Chapter Seven

Repairing a Shattered Spirit

Nevertheless, life has a funny way of moving on. I kept putting one foot in front of the other. And for a long time that seemed to work.

I attended both undergraduate and graduate school with the help of financial aid. It was one of the larger universities in the city, and I used public transportation along with a combination of other college students, high school students, and professionals going to and from work. I felt very grown up and independent, developing some higher education interests and successes in spite of the trauma of my childhood.

I found myself drawn to the courses that seemed to offer me release and resolution.

Besides the basic courses everyone had to take, I started taking other courses that both frightened me and strengthened me: Clinical Psychology, Sociology, Philosophy, Human Dynamics, and Abnormal Psychology just to name a few.

I took many of these courses at both the undergraduate and graduate levels. Each seemed to offer its own intensity academically, but also challenged my damaged spirit, as I was only a rookie beginning to understand the complexity of a sick mind.

I graduated from college now having a full six years of academics and clinical internships. As a Master's trained therapist, I had broad choices, and though I started working with children in a separate therapeutic arena, I eventually became certified in addictions counseling.

The training was grueling and I sought out supervision numerous times, due to my own unfinished grieving. I did not want my personal life to interfere with my work. I was able to achieve this for over a decade, until history started to repeat itself.

I met a kind, handsome, and supportive man. He had an easy demeanor and a warm smile. We enjoyed dinners in the city on weekends, and occasionally caught a hockey game. I thought of my dad at those times, but these moments were different.

After two years of dating, we started discussing marriage. Neither of us felt a strong urge to walk down the aisle, but we both wanted to have children. Our family values included marriage before children, so we moved forward with wedding plans.

We were married late in the afternoon, closer to early evening. The sun was setting and the sky was a magnificent combination of yellow, orange, and light shades of red. The temperature was perfect.

The weather was perfect and the event was perfect. Relatives, friends, and community members celebrated as we turned to a new chapter hoping to close the book on the past. I walked down the aisle to a song from West Side Story. "Somewhere." We truly hoped there was "a place for us," "a time for us," "a new way of living," and "a way of forgiving."

There was not a dry eye in the church. Many people knew of our family history, and my mother in particular was struggling to keep her composure.

We settled down in a suburb right outside the city and discussed starting a family. Since no professional had publicly taken a firm stance on genetics, we guessed our chances were fifty-fifty. Substance dependence ran on my husband's side, in addition to the mental illnesses on my side, so we sought genetics counseling multiple times. But no one seemed alarmed about mental illness or addiction. We were lulled into thinking that these were individual "problems," and we began feeling less worried and more encouraged. Maybe it really was less genetic and more environmental. We could not have been more tragically wrong.

In fact, over the course of having children, we continued to pursue genetics counseling. No counselor or medical provider seemed apprehensive. Were they speaking *lies in silence* or did they not know? This is a question that torments me often. We moved ahead with false belief and false hope, placing far too much confidence in providers and genetics counselors, who may not have had a clue about the awful truth. We placed our trust in them, which would become our most catastrophic and irreversible mistake.

My husband and I worked very hard to do everything "right." Car seats, outlet covers, and I nursed each child for at least a year. Private school, organic and healthy eating, and a house full of love. We played hide and go seek, spent long vacations together with other families, enjoyed backyard adventures hunting for bugs, went trick-or-treating, took long family bike rides, and had large barbeques and parties on Sunday after church.

We celebrated the simple things of life and we had enormous success as a family with the typical minor bumps. However, I never lost those apprehensive and anxious feelings. The constant worry I felt regarding my family's genetics and mine. I tried to ignore the feeling of doom that was to later be an ominous premonition.

Chapter Eight

Looming Genetics

It was in fourth grade, looking back, that there were subtle signs bubbling to the surface. Signs that could easily be interpreted as normal childhood development. But sadly it was not. With the help of available academic financial aid, our oldest daughter was in a private school setting, as we were sensitive to the need to provide a different childhood for our children than either of us had experienced.

During a routine meeting of several faculty members, one of the teachers stated her concerns for our daughter's inability to focus and sometimes sit still. "She is restless a lot, has a difficult time concentrating, and truthfully I wonder about ADHD. You may want to have her tested by a psychologist."

Since we were seeing no signs of this at all, her grades were always honor roll, she had an active social life, and was not creating problems, we dismissed this teacher's comments. We now know it is likely that the onset of illness was in fact at age nine.

The transition to middle school was difficult. After seven years in a small private school the transfer into a much larger public middle school was not easy for her. It was also at a time where her grandmother (my mother) was dying from a cancerous brain tumor

(Stage 3 Astrocytoma), so we started her in counseling to prevent what could become a deep sadness. Little did we know.

She liked her counselor, who recommended a small dose of an anti-depressant. We trusted this particular counselor so we agreed. Counseling and a small dose of medication seemed to hold her steady for school, activities, and eventually the funeral and burial of her beloved grandmother. After approximately six months she asked if she could stop taking the medication because she felt "better." She seemed better so we agreed, but kept her in counseling. It was a reasonable compromise.

Sometime later in middle school I received a phone call from one of the assistant principals asking if she could speak with me. She went on to tell me a story where our daughter had walked out of English class, and when asked by the teacher to return, she flat out refused. The assistant principal went on to say it was the "most severe case of defiance" she had ever seen. She sounded a bit melodramatic to me, and when we discussed the episode later that evening, an explanation was offered that sounded plausible. Could this be the normal acting out that accompanies adolescent development? Still not linking all of the pieces, we continued to live a normal life with no foresight of the freight train coming that was carrying mental illness for us all.

By the time she went to high school, it was more obvious that something else was going on. But again no big red flags until the night we learned she was thinking about swallowing a bottle of pills while my husband and I were out on a date. It was clear we needed to swiftly do something appropriate to the situation. After a lengthy, confusing conversation, she gave me permission to read her diary. It was filled with suicidal writings.

I shifted into clinician mode and I offered her three options. 1) Drive to the crisis center for an evaluation. 2) Talk about how she was feeling, in detail, with her dad and me. 3) Drive to Dunkin Donuts to get some hot cocoa and then decide the next step, the choices being numbers 1 or 2.

My thought at the time was that doing something normal, such as having hot chocolate with big fluffy marshmallows, would somehow change her mental status. I was looking to ease my own emotional pain and anxiety.

She voluntarily chose the crisis center. That was her first of six hospitalizations, each lasting less than a week. Initially she was prescribed an antidepressant, which at the time felt like the right decision.

After a couple of weeks on the medication, one night she provoked an argument with her dad and threw a lamp across the room. Having no history of violence, we were caught off guard by her behavior, quickly regrouping as she went running out the front door and down the street at eleven o'clock at night. Her feet were bare and she had a look in her eyes that was vaguely familiar to me. I chased after her, hearing my own heart pounding in my ears with fear and some awareness of what was happening.

After several hours of standing in the middle of our neighborhood under a pitch-black sky, I was able to convince her to walk to our porch. It was clear to me she was not in a normal state of mind.

We sat down on our front stoop, shoulder to shoulder, leaning on one another, while her dad retrieved two hand-made afghan blankets from the living room sofa. She was not rational. She was disoriented. Her eyes looked vacant and hollow. I knew. What *lies in silence* was no longer sleeping. It had come to claim my beautiful, kind, and sensitive daughter.

We sat there together for hours. The antidepressant, a medication effective for depression, was triggering a manic episode. She was fourteen, a freshman in high school, and entering the world of bipolar illness.

I was numb. I felt like I had swallowed a brick. My stomach hurt, my head hurt, but above all my heart had a throbbing ache that was familiar. I repressed the urge to vomit and quietly cried while we sat arm in arm, neither of us wanting to move or let go. She was scared of what was happening. I was terrified.

At one point, she turned to look at me and reached up to brush away one of my tears. "Don't cry, mom. It'll be okay." My heart sank. She didn't know.

Denial, shock, and overwhelming grief blocked our ability to understand how sick she was. This was our child. It couldn't be mental illness. Not again.

How could this be happening?

We did everything "right."

Someone should have warned us.

We were counseled and cautioned about Down's syndrome, neural tube defects, and general genetic defects.

Why not mental illness?

Why no genetics counseling for mental illness?

How could this be happening again?

How?

Chapter Nine

Suicide 101 — The Taboo Conversation

Tragically, our oldest child wasn't all right. She was the first born of the next generation, and was now part of our family legacy.

We watched while she suffered painful and excruciating symptoms, and observed constant judgment by others, while fighting hard for appropriate care via treatment and pharmaceuticals. Like millions of families this was our daily life, all while paying bills and trying to keep her safe. The form of disease she has does not seem to go into remission easily.

On one occasion, we openly discussed suicide. We had a very honest, as well as agonizing and difficult conversation. It was also a necessary conversation.

It was a short time after her first hospitalization while she was in the early stages of illness.

Suicide.

A taboo word and a taboo conversation.

Suicide.

Thoughts that come uninvited when you have a debilitating, life-threatening brain disease. A disease not helped by surgery. A disease not helped by an organ transplant.

Suicide.

A symptom of an internal imbalance in brain chemistry accompanied with an external bottomless grief. A symptom that occurs both inside and outside the movie theater in your head.

Why do people commit suicide?

Maybe a deep sense of desperation and sorrow unlike the myth of suicide being a selfish act. I suggest that suicide can be about ending your own pain while unintentionally inflicting pain upon others.

Suicide.

During an episode of full-blown psychosis or an unaware suicide, perhaps similar to a blackout.

Suicide.

Possibly from chronic misery and deep despair, unlike the myth that it stems from weakness or an act of cowardice.

Suicide.

I have reached a point in my professional and personal development where I don't believe all people choose suicide. I believe suicide chooses them.

The risk seemingly appears higher when there is an extreme level of physical, emotional, spiritual, and mental pain. There is desperation, absence of solutions, and the acute awareness of "coming to the end of the road." That's where suicide is waiting, at the end of the road, as a final solution to one's chronic suffering. Whether driven by psychosis or grief, the outcome is actually the same: tragedy.

Suicide comes as both an internal picture and an externally driven, overwhelming sense of loss, trauma, and grief. It happens when one's constant companions are loneliness and hopelessness.

It comes with the awareness that you are different or you feel broken and others choose to not be in your company. After all, you have a mood disorder and being in your own company is sometimes a challenge, as well. But you cannot stop being with yourself. Others can and they do. So your world shrinks: no one calls, no one sends flowers or email. They write you off. You become disposable and inferior and then you arrive at complete emotional bankruptcy.

Spiritually bankrupt. Emotionally bankrupt. Soulfully bankrupt. Bankrupt of hope and optimism, while dreams slip through your hands. All of these are ingredients for being a high risk for suicide. The idea that suicide is a conscious choice dismisses what occurs in a deeper, perhaps unrevealed part of the brain.

Never understanding suicide, I did now. It is one of those things that cannot be explained sufficiently unless you have had suicidal brain chemistry.

Ask anyone who has persistent and severe mental illness.

It feels as though it is the only way to end the pain, and it seems there are no other options for relief. You've tried them all. Multiple times.

Suicide.

Generated from inside the biochemical process as well as the external chronic woe and anguish.

On this occasion, my daughter and I were both prepared to have a very complicated conversation that was really not about suicide. It was about personal validation. Genuine. Authentic. Agonizing.

I whispered over to her sitting next to me in the car. "Will you let me know the next time you are suicidal?"

She sat thinking for a long moment and after carefully choosing her words, inhaled deeply, and then replied. "Only if you promise me that you won't rush me right over to the hospital."

She caught me off guard. She was being real. I had to step up. I was not sure I could make that promise. One of my cardinal rules was to never make promises in the world of mental health and addictions. Kept promises often cost people their lives. After attending many funerals of adolescents where promises were made and kept by others, it was not a request I took lightly. In addition to that, my life had already been shattered and riddled with tragedy and grief. I couldn't imagine this promise helping our situation.

I firmly gripped my sweaty palms around the steering wheel tightly enough to turn my knuckles white. The pain in my hands was a distraction from the searing pain and loud beating of my heart that was throbbing in my ears.

My response came slowly and thoughtfully. I was keenly aware of the implications of what I said and the potential outcome. I took a long, deep breath and replied.

"Well I'm willing to make you a deal. If you agree to come to me first when you are suicidal and we talk honestly and candidly, then we'll decide together if you should end your life. You. Me. Daddy."

I had not thought about how my husband would react to this very unconventional agreement with our daughter. In an instant, I decided we'd cross that bridge later.

She stared at me intensely. I could not see her but I could feel her gaze. It felt like it was burning into my cheek and I could not bring myself to look at her. If I glanced in her direction, I would either change my mind or begin to write her eulogy in my head. I knew at that very moment I could not afford to do either.

"What exactly are you saying, mom? Are you being serious? This is no time to make jokes or empty promises!" She started to get upset. I continued to look straight ahead so she could not see the pain in my eyes, nor sense the ache in my tired and wounded soul.

I felt like all the years of experience of counseling somehow prepared me for this moment in a cruel twist of fate. As I listened to clients and matured in my profession, I understood the symptom of suicide as a dual symptom — one that is experienced on both the inside and the outside. Similar to leprosy, as the illness has internal impact and external changes, bipolar often causes

permanent loss, grief, and stigma as the life one knew fades away.
Slips through the fingers like fine sand on a white beach.

I also learned that ego, arrogance, and self-righteousness often
got in the way, as many therapists lack the knowledge of how
suicide functions as a symptom of biochemical imbalance.

Most clients lack trust or faith that would allow them to discuss
the suicide process in a candid manner.

In health care there are also the obstacles of suicide protocols.
Family and friends sometimes have false belief that if they did
more, they could have persuaded the suffering person to stay.

But by far, the deepest travesty is when others assume they
understand another human being's personal journey through any
debilitating illness, most of all when it is a mental illness.

I whispered aloud in a coarse, dry voice, "If I cannot convince
you to stay and you still want to go because your suffering is so
great, then I will let you go. I won't interfere, even if I disagree. I
will never pretend that I understand your suffering. I don't. And
I'm very sorry that you are so sick, honey. I wish it were me
instead of you (an unintended premonition). I always feared getting
ill, but never in my most horrible nightmares could I have
imagined that your dad and I could create a beautiful child who'd
experience only suffering and loss."

One single tear rolled down my face.

She sat quietly while we both realized our conversation was something that no mother and daughter should ever have. Very quietly, she began to cry. A controlled and cleansing cry.

I realized then, only at that very moment, that I unknowingly gave her a gift rarely given. I validated her personal journey and her most painful life experience. No judgment. No shame. No stigma. Raw truth. She knew it, too. She whispered quietly, "It's a deal mom. Thank you." I exhaled. Incomprehensible mothering.

There was no parenting book for this. No child psychology and certainly no one to call and consult about such an honest, terrifying conversation. From a mother and daughter who'd had a love, a special love until a terrible illness came between them. I was on my own with this one. I felt alone and empty. She was already dying. Her life, her spirit, her soul, and her dreams were slipping away. And sadly we possessed no magical net to capture and hold the cherished parts of her that held her character and mission in life.

I thought of my father. She was on the same disastrous journey as the grandfather she had never met. And by virtue of our close family unit, we were now on it, too. Clinging to one another, knowing the outcome and her fate.

As I write this my thoughts turn to some of the misconceptions about suicide.

General misunderstanding. While suicides, as well as homicides, are sometimes acts of desperate individuals, statistics tell us that far more than 50% of those involved suffer from one or more mental illnesses. We must be willing to discuss both scenarios.

Some researchers suggest in families where there are generations of mental illness, there may also be multiple completed suicides and multiple tragedies driven by mental illness.

This is not to condone or offer support for anyone to knowingly or unknowingly commit suicide or to support any kind of violence. However, it is now clear to me why suicide (or having been chosen by suicide) becomes a final act to a chronic, painful, stigmatizing, and debilitating daily life of unimaginable suffering.

Both a symptom of brain disease and an act of ending sorrow that is unexplainable, it is a desperate escape from pain, loss, and judgment. It is a way to permanently put an end to shattered dreams, broken relationships, deadly addictions, years of life lost in prison, shame, embarrassment, and stigma. Always stigma.

A routine where there is no joy, no friendship, and only pain and isolation.

Perhaps people will start to grasp suicide for what it is. It may be a difficult, painful act. An action as honest and excruciating as speaking with a strong voice, while validating and tragically letting go of a daughter in a moment where she needs to feel heard.

An understanding that in spite of all you do, it is still possible that in the end the disease and the person who is suffering are left unstable, symptomatic, and disabled; in addition to many families with completed suicide as part of their family legacy. Pure powerlessness. No different from Romeo and Juliet, Love Story, *or* Brian's Song. *Tragic. Final. Permanent.*

Chapter Ten

Endless Judgment

At every meeting we attended at school, whether it was for a 504 Plan or an Individualized Educational Plan (both which are used for academic assistance), we were met with uneducated and judgmental looks. These were professionals who assessed our oldest daughter as having the intelligence to do the work, though they lacked knowledge about how her mental illness greatly impacted the learning process. Guidance counselors and administrators constantly looked at us with judgmental and piercing stares, but never understanding or asking in order to offer support rather than added stress.

One guidance counselor, in particular, was exceptionally inappropriate. Once when our oldest daughter was attempting to cope with her symptoms of agitation, anxiety, and unstable brain chemistry with some superficial cutting of her wrists, he decided his intervention would somehow jolt her into behaving differently. The timing was soon after she attended a day treatment program.

The guidance counselor was trained in academic counseling. He was very young and lacked maturity or sophistication and was not educated about mental illness. He did not understand her suffering. The perfect circumstances for stigma. He minced no words as we sat there exhausted, grieving, and defeated. In a cocky and condescending manner he started the meeting. "I see you learned some new tricks while you were in treatment," he said to our daughter, referring to the recent incident where she had purposely cut herself on the wrist.

His flip attitude was a reminder of how uneducated and cruel the world can be toward the mentally ill. He took the liberty, in a public forum, to verbally assault a child, moving forward on his own agenda without even trying to understand the situation.

This was a young man with absolutely no information on mental illness. But like many others, arrogance plus ignorance somehow gave him permission to insult a mentally ill student — as though what he was proposing was some kind of divine insight. He continued to be ineffective in helping us due to his closed-minded and narrow thinking. He asked no questions regarding her diagnosis, her symptom profile, her suffering, nor a gesture toward seeking extra academic support. It was as though she had become a leper overnight. We wound up going over his head rather than adding another layer of burden to an already overstressed situation.

This incident spoke volumes of the hurt we knew was only a glimpse of what would be the new life for her. My husband reached for my hand under the table. I became very tearful and the psychologist who'd fought for us in the past firmly silenced the guidance counselor. She was extraordinary and I sensed that on many levels she did get it.

Special education costs school districts a lot of money. At times administrators appeared to assess whether she was really sick, as this is an invisible disability and *lies in silence*. The assessments often appeared to be based on dollars rather than illness. A culture seen often in attempting to secure appropriate level of care while someone else holds the dollars needed and the ultimate decision.

Were it not for the school psychologist, we would have had no one to advocate for our daughter in the meeting. No one with authority willing and competent to raise their voice in a meeting, where parents are dismissed as inadequate and somehow responsible for the student's inability to achieve. Even so, these twice-a-year meetings proved to be a breeding ground for politics, money, and unsolicited opinions on mental health, our parenting style, and our limit-setting ability.

In addition to routine school meetings where we faced a table full of stares and indifference, we found that other routine and regular events were also affected in ways that caused even more stress and vulnerability.

Halloween, typically an innocent neighborhood event of costumes and candy, was now stressful and risky. Being out late at night in the dark while adorable, creative, and sometimes scary children go door to door became a family holiday where I now walked on pins and needles.

Would the paranoia stay in check?

How would my children decipher the difference between neighbors in costume versus visual hallucinations or pictures from within their minds?

How do we greet the neighbors?

Who among them had seen the police cars in our driveway?

The worries were now endless.

Fourth of July, though a summer celebration in the past, now brought concerns similar to Halloween. The added risks were from the bright flashes of light in the sky that could stimulate unstable brain chemistry and the noise of firecrackers and large fireworks, all increasing the risk of a child going into a public rage.

And then there was the chronic and predictable issue of the full moon. Occurring once a month, with an almost 100% guarantee that there would be a surge of symptoms typically acute and severe. Every single full moon. A phenomenon not fully understood, but agreed by many, appears to potentially be a brain-triggering and predictable event.

We elected to hang up a special calendar indicating the phases of the moon. Our family used to enjoy a full moon, sometimes roasting marshmallows over our backyard campfire or making s'mores. We now dreaded the full moon.

Daily we struggled with the simple event of getting our oldest daughter out of bed and to school. Due to the cycle of her mood disorder, her brain was programmed to chronic insomnia, and then, once finally asleep, she was unable to awaken in the morning. No matter what creative intervention we tried, it was impossible to get her to school.

Our jobs were in jeopardy as we scrambled to devise a plan every morning, and most school years she had over fifty absences and more than twenty tardies. The woman in charge of attendance and the administrator were not educated about mental illness or disordered sleep, and they were unforgiving and rigid on a daily basis. These absences and chronic tardiness were due to mental illness, not truancy. They were uninterested in the reasons and only cared about the broken code of student conduct.

Once in school, the intense lights effective for learning and studying contributed to an environment already difficult to negotiate, seeming to trigger activation in her brain.

Like an incubator stimulating life in newborn babies or chickens, this incubator stimulated perilous brain activation. The loud sounds of students in the hall, the normal roar typical in every school setting, and the horrible secret she carried that she was, in fact, mentally ill. It made her unstable and different.

How could it not?

I watched my oldest daughter continue to suffer tremendously from both physical and emotional pain. She, like my father in the generation before me, was unable to maintain friendships and had long, deep depressions that lasted for entire school years.

She lost all confidence and all faith in adults, blaming us for her illness. For years I accepted that blame, feeling I should not have trusted others and their *lies in silence*, when my gut instinct told me differently. Blame I continue to struggle with as our nightmare continues.

She'd reprimand us multiple times and emphatically stated that we should have never had children with a family history of mood disorders and addiction on both sides. We had no answers for her. In many ways, she was right. However, we were incorrectly informed. That was little consolation for her.

My husband's side of the family had mentioned there were several family members with alcoholism, and much later we found out there was a completed suicide that was NEVER discussed. There was no connection made decades ago about the potential relationship between mental disorders and addiction. If we'd known, we may have made the decision to do further research before having children.

In addition, had we been faced with accurate information, it is possible we would have ignored it and taken the often-traveled path of "it won't happen to us." Or we might have made a decision to grow old without children and somehow learn to live without children in a world that seems focused on babies, toddlers, and childhood.

At the same time she was blaming us, her life continued to spiral out of control in an avalanche of mental health symptoms. She had no identity development as her brain swirled day in and day out. Her moods swung from one extreme to the other and she suffered horrific side effects as we searched for medications to offer her any possible relief.

She had worked hard in school, earning honor roll, and participated in cheerleading during the years she was stable. But regardless of our conscientious and aggressive attempts, every spring she became wildly manic.

One spring her squad was attending a national competition. It was in the month of March, one of the worst times of the year for her. At the last minute, we could not let her go. We could not expect her coaches or the chaperones to monitor a child with this level of mental illness.

She was devastated and inconsolable as she'd practiced for three years with this squad, and they had planned for this trip a full year in advance. This was another loss for her, but this only represented her personal mounting losses in a larger, more hopeless manner. This demonstrated for her in one crushing blow that she was losing everything that mattered. She was sixteen years old.

My husband and I had no words of wisdom. One of our many parenting moments where there was nothing to say pertaining to comfort and loss. It speaks for itself, and it was one of the many lessons when we learned that love was not enough. Life was slipping through her hands. It was gut-wrenching for all of us. We had all worked hard and had made so many sacrifices. Nevertheless, the heartache and sadness continued to multiply.

Chapter Eleven

Hypersexuality

Our oldest daughter continued to experience abnormal and excruciating suffering in high school, and in her senior year she had her first truly full-blown manic episode, a talking-on-the-telephone-until-five-in-the-morning type of episode.

Our previously warm and safe home was transformed into a psychiatric unit, and monitoring was now required 24 hours a day, seven days a week. Nothing was out of the question, as we quickly found out in our crash course of parenting a manic child. We had heard stories, and the bulk of the stories or families I treated described adolescent mania to be a harrowing, frightening, maddening, exhausting, disheartening experience.

Jumping out of moving cars, leaving the house at all hours of the night, moving from one group of mentally ill teens to another, seeking the end to pain and suffering not understood by most adults.

She spent the entire evening awake, in a mental state that is indescribable to others unless it's been an uninvited presence in your home. She was in and out of the kitchen all night long, sometimes cooking full meals, slamming pantry doors and the refrigerator door looking for something in particular. In the morning and throughout the day we'd find empty wrappers, trash, plates, cups, and the remnants of the last feeding frenzy. We stopped buying certain items and made some attempts to hide the groceries. No matter how often we asked her to clean up after herself, it never occurred. This was not our daughter. Our daughter had great hygiene, was helpful around the house, and was thoughtful of others. This was her illness making its presence known.

Several times we drug tested her, and each time it was negative. In some ways it was a discouraging result as it confirmed that this was full-blown mental illness.

We heard constant, non-stop, pressured talking on the telephone in a loud and piercing voice, in a dramatic and rapid-fire manner. She moved from one television to the other, letting them blare with no recognition of others sleeping in the house. And at times, she would text message late into the night with people we did not know. On one occasion, as she slept, I took her cell phone to read the message at 3 AM in the morning. It was the name of a male, and the conversation was graphically sexual in nature. This confirmed our suspicion. She was severely hypersexual during this phase of unstable mood. I became more frightened for her safety, for the risk of sexually transmitted diseases, for the risk of pregnancy, and the risk of being seduced by someone who she would believe would take her away from this pain and suffering. This was a page out of my sister's book of illness.

We began shutting down access to technology in a futile attempt to keep her safe. We disconnected her cell phone, something we had gotten merely to keep track of her. We blocked some of the computer services, but kept her instant messaging so we could monitor her level of instability. One of our fears was that she would meet someone online and leave the state.

Prom, graduation, and college acceptance letters turned into running the streets, stealing our car, threatening to hurt other peers, unknown cars and drivers outside our home, and hypersexuality. She was medicated. This was active disease.

Hypersexuality, described by many as multiple and frequent sex acts with one person or frequent sex acts with multiple partners.

Hypersexuality, like having a pornographic XXX film playing on the movie screen inside your head. This was now the *Hypersexuality Movie Theater*.

Frightening and scary like a sexual horror picture, as most of the images are considered deviant, abnormal, and sick. They are intrusive thoughts that occur anywhere. Sitting in a classroom, being at work, driving in a car, or while talking to a doctor. They are insidious and random.

Hypersexuality, as a symptom, is difficult to discuss because most people cannot grasp this symptom without passing judgment.

And sadly, it seems many professionals lack insight into this, due to some accompanying issues, such as sexually transmitted diseases, pregnancy, and what is imprecisely described as promiscuity. It presents itself in varied ways.

From putting a porn picture on the windshield of a car, to being in a dumpster for a three way, to going on porn sites, to engaging in online sex chats with people claiming to be heterosexual, homosexual, or bisexual. These symptoms typically only presented during periods of hypomania or her mixed states.

There were also slight indications of it: wanting to lie on top of someone in the home, dressing inappropriately, and an increase in sexualized conversation.

Our daughter would not discuss her symptom of hypersexuality with a therapist or with us. She said it was too risky because after a manic episode that included hypersexuality, she felt her behavior was shameful and embarrassing, and her level of regret was enormous.

It was a striking change from an honor roll student, church youth group leader, successful part-time employee, cheerleader, family-centered, accepted into first choice college, beautiful, funny, loving, and talented young woman. She was now becoming like her grandfather, and her aunts and uncle, exhibiting many of the same symptoms they displayed during their own experience of illness. The disease was extinguishing my daughter just as it had taken my father and others in what was my family.

Why?

How?

When our daughter is manic, she resists help and creates enormous chaos in our home. Her second manic episode was triggered by a low dose birth control pill, recommended by her physician to regulate menstruation.

Since starting medication for bipolar, she had never had a normal menstrual cycle. This idea was meant to be beneficial. However, it caused a spiraling out of control, dangerous, and insane roller coaster ride of enormous proportion.

Our other daughter, at the same time was having extreme bouts of paranoia, so frightened at times that she refused to shower. Though well medicated, this was one of the symptoms that has been relentless.

She has also shown significant signs of hypersexuality like her older sister, as we discovered while checking our computer spyware one night. The sites she visited were not normal adolescent interests, and we sadly realized it was something else.

Yet when we attempted to discuss this with her, she stated she "could not remember" visiting those sites. Something an adolescent would say. These sites were different. We became severely worried. More worry on top of worry.

Was my dad "not aware" of his behavior because of this illness?

Would everyone have lapses in memory during active episodes?

We shuddered to think of multiple family members not having awareness of their behavior, yet in some ways that made the most sense.

We didn't have a chance against this illness. I became disheartened and emotionally despondent.

Chapter Twelve

Piercing a Dying Heart

We took our oldest daughter to another psychologist for a risk assessment in order to get her back into school following one of her extended times in treatment. How could I not have known? Was my denial that pervasive?

My daughter could not be as sick as some of the kids I have seen. Could she?

I am still not sure what kept me so stuck, but if I had to take a guess, it would be my family history and, more specifically, my father. If my daughter was like my father, would she murder other people? Would she kill herself?

Though I did not know the answers to these questions, I became obsessed with her. Her life. Her death. Her. I was not going to let another person I loved get swallowed by mental illness. And for sure not one of my children.

And though this was more than any human being should ever endure, it was not yet over. Genetics that *lie in silence* had now set their focus on the rest of my children, and ultimately me.

It was the month of March, when the tidal wave consumed the rest of my family. I had felt that the worst was behind me. I was undeniably wrong.

It was at one of the times when dad's story was mentioned publicly, just three years after our oldest daughter was diagnosed, when our genetics were triggered again and voraciously swallowed the rest of the people I love.

Our son was triggered into a manic episode, at the age of three, after being treated with a steroid for pneumonia. In addition, our middle daughter, suffering from anxiety for a year, began having severe paranoia again.

While experiencing shock and deep despair, and feeling overcome with grief watching my innocent children slip away, I was catapulted into the world of bipolar by a migraine prevention medication.

It was reprehensible that my neurologist had not researched mood-triggering medications. She knew about my family history. She was willing to take the risk of trading migraine headaches for a lifetime sentence of mental illness. A risk she took with my brain.

It was too late for me now. The damage was done.

Permanent damage. It was an overwhelming turn of events and this all took place over a few days. Days. A few days. I remember the moment like the moment I was told about the terrorist attacks on 9/11, like the day I was told about my father's horrific homicide/suicide, like the day we packed the car and left the life we once knew. It was an experience that is forever painted on the canvas of my mind.

The weekend we all got sick is something that will never leave my psyche. There were multiple things happening and the level of stress was crushing. It was yet another scenario creating levels of post-traumatic stress disorder, severe mental health symptoms, and the deepest level of loss and grief that only one who has been through it can know. This was the deadly cluster of circumstance now known by another generation. I was unable to move physically, and for the first time ever in my life I knew I had no resources to address the slow death of my family...again.

It began early one Saturday morning while I was on the telephone speaking to our oldest daughter who had taken (stolen) our car overnight without permission. Mid-conversation I felt a tremendous, massive snap in my brain. A snap similar to forcefully pulling on someone's suspenders and then snapping them back in place. Within seconds I felt all of the air, the energy, and the life leave my body, starting at the brain and flowing like an undertow or unstoppable flood of water down my entire body and out through my feet.

From that moment on, after the snap in my brain and every night since, my pattern of sleep has never been normal. Never.

I can no longer fall asleep on my own, nor stay asleep, after never before having sleep issues. I knew what this was. This was sleep dysregulation. The part of my brain that created regular sleep patterns was now broken. Similar to a wind-up clock, the pieces of my clock were now permanently not working. Initially, at the onset of my illness, I did not sleep for three weeks. (That's 504 hours or 30,240 minutes or 1,814,400 seconds.) There are no words to adequately describe this constant state of physical, mental, and emotional pain, most of it spent alone.

During those three weeks, as the nights passed with unrelenting wakefulness, I did little but speed channel surfing, with no purpose other than getting away from the internal process in my mind.

I was suffering from severe anhedonia, also known as lack of pleasure.

---

anhedonia: a psychological condition characterized by inability to experience pleasure in normally pleasurable acts

---

Since I derived simple pleasure for the majority of my life, I recognized this symptom as well. No joy. Lack of experiencing pleasure in anything.

I decided to get what I thought would be temporary sleep medication. I was unable to get an appointment with a psychiatrist for two months, and the crisis center had already misdiagnosed me once. But I intuitively knew if I did not sleep soon, I would likely have a full psychotic break. I would become my father.

So, the next day I made an appointment with my primary care physician, the kind of doctor who is great for strep throat, bronchitis, and high cholesterol. She was clearly confused about me. My chart had many papers accumulated over a decade of infrequent primary care visits, but there was no documentation or clinical notes about mental illness, sleep problems, or psychiatric history.

There was no documentation because I had no prior history of mental illness. I quietly requested sleep medication while she continued to visually assess me. I felt ashamed for many reasons, and the look of judgment on her face was not reassuring.

I had not showered in weeks, my hair was loosely pulled back in a hair band, and I wore no make up. I was unrecognizable to anyone who knew me.

My physician was evaluating me in a manner familiar to me, as I had done similar clinical assessments for over twenty-five years. She was trying to determine whether I was drug seeking — a term we use in the drug and alcohol counseling field for clients who are addicted to prescription drugs and see multiple physicians in order to get multiple prescriptions.

I did not know what to say to assure her. My request was only for some sleeping medicine, not for something to alter my mood or feed an addiction. I knew if I asked her what she was thinking, she would most likely not give me an honest answer. I felt humble in a sick and shameful way. I did not want to beg, but the thought of becoming psychotic after all I had been through was too much to bear. This was not a physician who I'd known for years, as my primary internist had left months before. And, truthfully, there was no record because I had not been mentally ill until now.

This came on her watch, so to speak. I felt badly for her, ironically, but not that badly. I was not leaving her office without a prescription. I would plead if it was necessary, and the thought of begging quickly brought tears to my eyes, and created a large lump in my throat. I was at my breaking point.

The doctor's face had stigma plastered all over it like a neon sign in the middle of the night. It was my first profound incident of stigma, and I learned this would be my most unwanted, constant companion for the rest of my life. I found a morsel of advocacy to speak and I firmly said, "Look, can you just give me enough sleep meds until I see the psychiatrist? I am not functioning at all, I have some pretty scary stuff going on in my head, and I have mentally ill children to care for."

She merely nodded her head showing no compassion or interest in my newfound suffering. She carefully prescribed six sleeping pills. They were a class of sleeping medication and strength that I knew would be unlikely to give me any relief. But I took them out of sheer desperation, as my options of preventing psychosis were dwindling day by day.

The pills allowed me to sleep 1-2 hours per night. It was enough to increase my chances of not becoming my dad. This was a daunting and sinking reminder of the thin line between sanity and insanity. I took a deep breath. I instinctively knew this was the first of many obstacles to come.

I lay in bed, unable to move, suffering from my first suicidal major depressive episode. The physical and emotional soreness and body aches were agonizing. Similar to the flu with the volume button turned up to a screaming level, thousands of decibels higher than any routine virus or flu.

This was a depression so deep and so painful, I realized for the first time that the pain of this illness cannot possibly be known by those who do not suffer. I became one of the knowing. I was now a member of an elite club of sufferers who do not dare to speak the worst symptoms of all, due to fear of more stigma and forced institutionalization.

I felt sad. I felt immobilized and there was no one to tell. I could only tell myself. And myself was no longer competent. It was a dead end and a circular dilemma. At the moment, I saw no way out. I was trapped in my head and with children of all ages trapped in their heads. We were prisoners, finding little compassion or interest from the usual resources in our mentally healthy lives. I began to cry.

It all was just too much. Getting up for even a moment was painful. Tears ran down my face. All I could see was that we were all turning into my father. I felt the room spin as a surge of nausea wracked my beleaguered body. I slid onto the floor.

Lying on the floor I asked myself, how much could one family endure?

And then I whispered out loud, while sobbing and rocking, "Why are you taking my children away?"

Why are you taking my children away?!

WHY ARE YOU TAKING MY CHILDREN AWAY??!

WHY ARE YOU TAKING MY CHILDREN AWAY???!!

With each question, the volume of my voice, a voice I did not recognize, grew louder and louder until I was screaming while rolling on the floor. Waves of tears fell from my eyes as I shook and beat on my chest. It was an involuntary and uncontrollable expression of the depth of my grief. It was symbolic of the loss of my children, the loss of my family, and the loss of natural motherhood — a role that partially defined my purpose and brought simple joy to my daily life.

This was a mother's dramatic expression of the deepest grief there is: losing a child. I thought of my grandmother lying on her son's casket in church. I thought of my dad and his loss of fatherhood and the life he'd built with my mother. I thought of my mother and how she lost a magical relationship and her children (my siblings). I was the next in line. My losses were no different. Perhaps the only difference was that I was fully aware of the genetic destruction, therefore perhaps having a greater desire to end the suffering from what *lies in silence.*

There are millions of families like mine. I think about the many clients over the years that undoubtedly had similar severe mental illness. The millions who lie in silence *and remain voiceless, suffering from addictions to gambling, drugs, alcohol, shopping, food, and sex.*

Those in our legal system housed in deplorable conditions, while suffering from severe symptoms like ours. An epidemic growing stronger and larger, while taking hostages younger and younger.

A disease seeming to exist undeniably from birth to death.

All this while the country that I love, my family loves, my father loved, and my grandparents immigrated to from thousands of miles away sits by, responding in insufficient ways, telling lies in silence.

There have been widespread cuts in services, leaving mental health organizations bleeding out. Some drug reps and some psychiatrists have made unethical alliances with one another, having conferences in the Bahamas and Fiji, worrying more about their bottom line than the suffering of millions. Headlines scream about billions of dollars in profits while necessary medications remain unaffordable to the neediest consumers.

Several reputable mental health research organizations released figures showing that in 2004 suicide was the 11th leading cause of death in the United States, third among individuals 15-24.

I felt more hopeless. I felt more bitter. I felt more angry. I felt more resentful. We were the forgotten. Deserted. I started to cry again. Quiet sobbing so I wouldn't scare my children, my very sick children, who could also potentially hurt themselves or others.

How will we know?

Though not everyone with mental illness self-injures or hurts others, these symptoms can be chronic, acute, and debilitating. I felt strongly that we had to find a way to discuss the spectrum of mood disorders, recognizing that some with unstable mood become violent, while others seemingly never do. Living in a society where everything needs a category, it was obvious why those with mood disorders elected silence.

Who among us wants to be known as a future murderer?

Would I choose silence because of my family history?

Our lives changed permanently, exactly like my childhood, but far worse. No more soccer practice, games, or weekend tournaments. No more gymnastics and no summer camp. We now needed special education with every academic accommodation available. No more summers at the beach, no swimming lessons, no drum lessons, and no normal living.

Our monthly intake of prescription drugs now topped twenty-seven different medications and, without two separate areas of medical coverage, we would be forced to suffer more restrictions of basic needs such as shelter and food.

This all while a medical community only whispers the warning, and lies in silence, while some pharmaceutical companies advertise openly that they quadrupled revenue and profit margins for drugs used for mental illness.

And there are more lies. Drug testing is full of misrepresentations, bad science, payments from drug companies to researchers, lies, or exaggerations about the significance of the effects that are seen, and side effects that are swept under the rug. Meds are used in circumstances they were never tested for, especially with children. Some of the medications cause the disease to get worse.

I don't understand.

Does this not speak to the issue of inattentiveness in the medical community during an emerging epidemic? Who fell asleep at the wheel?

I thought of the women like me throughout the world. It's hard to forget the vivid images of mothers and fathers on the news, holding their children in their arms, while crumbling to the ground under the emotional burden of their death. Many of them from war-torn and third world countries; many from American streets where shootings, violence, suicide, and murder take sons and daughters every day. These are searing images for any parent as they watch the uncontrollable sobbing of other parents, beating on their chests expressing their grief from losing their child.

Which generation would I grieve first? My children, my siblings, myself, my father? Do I grieve for them as though a minivan has been demolished in a violent car crash and incinerated by a fire, killing all of them? How do you grieve for so many at once? How do you grieve while others judge?

It was at that very moment that I had a flashback. It was about an article written by several reporters after stalking and then speaking to members of our church. The reporters wrote that one of the church members inside at the time told them that dad was asking the minister questions. It was the memory of my father standing and questioning our minister. Dad was shouting then whispering. I was whispering then shouting. The question was the same. The answer was a deep echoing silence.

And then a bone-chilling question crossed my mind, *I wonder if I could hurt people.*

Collapsed on the bathroom floor, crying and vomiting, I finally had the full emotional picture of what my family had become. It didn't matter that we had done everything right. We lost. The flawed genetics had won. It was only a matter of time. I continued to kneel over the toilet.

For months, my husband had to make me a list to take grocery shopping. Without the list, I wandered around the store for hours. Though I sensed I was wandering, the fog in my brain kept me disoriented and confused enough that I could not locate groceries, place them in a shopping cart, and proceed to the checkout line as I had for decades.

I feared running into anyone I knew, but there was so little I could do at home I felt obligated to continue this one weekly task. Driving was risky, working was difficult, and had we not desperately needed the money, I would have considered taking a leave of absence.

I kept the therapy sessions for my clients as basic as I could, losing some of the cognitive and therapeutic skills required for helping others to recover from multiple addictions, cope with mental health disorders, and traumatic life events. The section in my brain in charge of abstract and critical thinking was not available to me while unstable. It was evident and devastating when I read back over my notes, staring down at rambling sentences that were not sequential, and were sadly indicative of my mental status. These were skills arduously developed over many years of my professional career. It was symbolic of how broadly efficient the illness had become.

I also lost my ability to cook. After the third time I started a small fire in the kitchen, we decided I shouldn't cook until some of my long-term memory was accessible.

Much of my brain and memory had been affected. I was unable to do the most simple of tasks regardless of my graduate school degree and regardless of decades of cooking experience. Yet another loss.

The illness seemed to override a large section of my thinking and my ability to perform basic tasks. What I missed the most, though, was the ability to share in relationships and experience life's simple joys. I no longer felt pure joy. I lost interest in dancing, music, old movies, and I could no longer sing. My voice could not hold a pitch and I sang out of tune. So, I stopped singing. I had enjoyed singing for decades and on occasion joined a choir or musical theater group. The illness was now taking my voice. The goal seemed to make me *lie in silence*. The question was would I?

I loved dancing my entire life. I had taken dance lessons up until my father's death, and I often went dancing with a group of friends. I no longer enjoyed music. I lost the desire to listen to music I'd listened to for years.

Was there anything left to take?

There was.

The smell of a flower, the feel of the warm sun on my face, the giggle of my children, a fresh hot cup of hazelnut coffee, cold chocolate water ice, a good family movie, the wind blowing in my hair, the sound of crickets at night, a beautiful warm fire, or hot pizza with extra cheese. Pure joy was gone. I felt dead. Dead while still living. Severe, chronic, and persistent illness brings despair. I was becoming educated about a world I'd never known. A world where millions suffer daily. A world where the best one can hope for is respite or remission. I was overwhelmed by the drastic changes. Changes that came with no notice, no preparation, and no directions. Changes that were permanent.

Chapter Thirteen

Suicidal Movie Theater

While the pain was making itself at home in my body, an unending, continuous movie scrolled across my thought screen, playing variations of methods to commit suicide. It reminded me of the small planes that pull banners at the beach advertising restaurants and beer. However, these banners advertised types of suicide. It was absolutely horrifying.

This was a suicidal movie theater in my mind. A theater with no doors to leave and a motion picture on the reel that never stops rolling. No director to yell cut. No hot buttered popcorn, no box of snowcaps, no gummy bears, and no nachos with cheese.

This film played pictures of jumping off of a bridge, overdosing on bottles of pills, hanging myself with a thick and twisted rope, driving into the path of an eighteen-wheel truck barreling down the highway, shooting myself in the head with a handgun, slitting my throat with a large kitchen knife, and sitting in my running car in the closed garage.

These pictures played like a slide show where the finger rests on the forward button, so pictures flash quickly, as if one is looking for a certain slide to show friends, like photos of your latest vacation. It is a finger not identifiable and not within reach. The movie frames came in and out of my internal screen at a rapid pace, as is the common identifier of racing and random suicidal thoughts. They were vivid, gory, and frightening.

There was no mistaking what this was. It was inside, not outside. I could not make it stop. Whether my eyes were open or closed, the pictures remained. They were pictures manufactured and projected in my brain. It was like watching a horror movie with no way out of the theater while sitting frightened and panicked.

What *Lies In Silence* — Or Whom?

Bipolar Disorder Returns — The Next Generation (The Mini Series)

Suicide for Dummies

This was biochemical and I could not make the bloody pictures go away. I had never been suicidal in my life, but this was easy to differentiate from any other symptom. I was experiencing racing suicidal thoughts created by my new mental illness.

I felt a deep wave of nausea. At the age of forty-three, ironically one year shy of my father's age when he committed murder/suicide, I now suffered from bipolar disorder triggered by a medication prescribed for preventing migraines. This was my new genetic status, a complimentary memento from a mood-triggering medication.

But even more frightening was that I now personally knew the depth and extent of the all-encompassing mental and physical torture experienced on a daily basis by my children, my father, my siblings, my aunts, uncles, cousins, and my clients. I was now one of them. I was overcome with hopelessness and a deep sense of sorrow.

One evening, at a time when I was besieged with chilling bloody pictures running rapidly through my mind, I lay motionless in our bed unable to move any part of my body.

Sometime after my husband and the kids ate dinner, our ten-year-old daughter ran down the hall and into the master bedroom. She was screaming, frightened by a feeling that someone was watching her, while at the same time having a vision of a bearded man, all of this manufactured by her brain. She dragged her sleeping bag along with her, as she entered my room and settled herself on the floor next to my side of the bed. I whispered to her to hang on and we would try to make the scary man go away with an increase in medication.

I began to cry because our situation was now becoming more than we could handle. And the horror of my own pain was nothing compared to the heartache of watching my children become mentally ill members of the club. I knew their lives would likely be one loss and torture after another.

Interrupting my gloomy thoughts, one minute later, maybe two, our three-year-old son dashed into our bedroom, quickly hopped onto the bed, and crawled under the blanket as if to snuggle with me. He wiggled his small, round face into the crook of my neck and in a soft whisper that felt warm like a gentle breeze he said, "Mommy please make the voices go away."

It was at that moment that I suffered what I can only term as irreconcilable trauma and grief. I had now lost everyone I loved. I closed my eyes and begged to die. I thought of my father. I got it. I understood. I was overwhelmed.

IT'S GENETICS!

IT'S GENETICS!

IT'S GENETICS!

I surrendered. Bipolar had won.

I gently tried to tell my husband and our other family members assisting us at this time, but no one could grasp the idea that mental illness now consumed our toddler. He had already been showing signs of other co-occurring disorders, possibly attention deficit/

hyperactivity disorder. It was difficult to have a reliable differential diagnosis as his mood was not stable, and it was vital to be accurate since the treatment for hypomania can be devastating if treated as ADHD.

Though he had experienced signs of hypomania recently triggered by a steroid medication, he had never suffered from auditory hallucinations. As sick as I was, I knew I had to determine if this was active disease or a paradoxical medication effect. This was a daunting task, as the controversy in the medical community, as well as the general population, grows in regards to mental health treatment and the use of medication for toddlers.

It remains an impossible undertaking. And sadly, in addition to his unstable mood, he had very clear signs of obsessive-compulsive disorder, evidenced by routine counting, significant rituals around mealtime, rituals around putting his shoes and socks on, rituals at bedtime regarding brushing his teeth a certain way, the order of occurrence, and other signs only noticed by his dad and me. We found out much later that his need to "touch back" after being touched was not a typical child's reaction to the game "I got you – I got you last." It was, in fact, according to the official diagnostic tool, part of a ritual of OCD. We were incredibly saddened after reading this credible assessment tool.

And yet the doubt of what we said was palpable. Doctors and psychologists did not believe it was as bad as we described, and a few contradicted what we said by spouting statistics about age of onset of mental health disorders.

Why in the world would we make this stuff up about our three year old?

So we knew it was unlikely a provider would know, or know enough, to be of any help to our family. They would not check thyroid numbers. They most likely would not think a medication for unstable mood could trigger a psychotic reaction.

However, I knew differently. I had spent four years doing research once our oldest daughter was triggered. I had a false sense of hope I could save her. But I was wrong. We considered an evaluation with an expert in the field of pediatric bipolar disorder and co-occurring disorders, but it seemed that all of them had gone to private pay with no access to service via a sliding scale, denying treatment for the youngest victims of the disease. Treatment for the victims they profess to care about was now only affordable for the wealthy. We were already stretched to our breaking point. It was not an option financially, and ethically I struggled with the moral implications of this style of providing service, let alone participating and supporting it with our dwindling income.

Our oldest daughter had experienced quite a few offending meds, and some of them took weeks to activate what is termed a paradoxical reaction. The longer it took to trigger this type of reaction, the higher the risk for the worst-case scenario. She missed many days of school with these medication trials and paradoxical effects came often.

I sobbed and sobbed uncontrollably with each child I had to medicate. With each mood stabilizer and each atypical antipsychotic the sobbing was more pronounced. Deep, heavy, and uncontrollable sobbing. My heart was irreparably shattered. I felt cold, numb, and dead inside.

I had failed to protect my children from the silent, deep-seated, destructive gene in our family. I did not know what *lies in silence* for it hibernated within me, and I unknowingly passed it on. More family members sent to the mental illness death camp.

My husband and I set up safety precautions all over the house. We now had motion monitors for all of the doors and the garage. We needed large pillbox containers for pharmaceuticals, and eventually we had to fill out multiple applications for medical assistance, one for each child. I thought of my mother sitting on her bed filling out state aid forms such as medical assistance, welfare benefits that included food stamps and cash assistance, while weeping quietly to herself. My chest felt tight, I couldn't breathe, and I was suddenly light-headed.

We discussed for weeks putting an alarm system in the whole house, more to prevent catastrophe from the inside, rather than prevent criminals from the outside.

There were three ways to get in and out of the house, and after our oldest daughter left in the middle of the night with the car and our son got a stool from the kitchen and let himself out through the front door, it became evident that the choice was made for us.

Although we had "reasonable" private insurance, the financial cost of this much mental illness was draining our budget. We were already beginning to drown in every aspect of our life.

I experienced overwhelming sadness and anger. We were the next two generations.

Unthinkable.

Unbelievable.

Inconceivable.

Incomprehensible.

How long would these drugs keep my children's minds quiet?

Would they give them a better chance?

Was I prolonging the inevitable and raising children who would eventually take their own lives or the life of someone else?

Would others insult us and call us cruel and hurtful names?

Do we have credibility in spite of now having diseased brains?

Do others think our character is flawed so we *lie in silence*?

Where were the powerful, influential, and candid voices of the medical community on this epidemic?

I felt invisible, mute, and hopeless. I could not manage this. But the alternative was drastic. My kids would then know my childhood. I could not leave my husband to care for three mentally ill children on his own. For now, I had to stay. The decision to live was difficult. Moreover, ultimately I knew I stayed to not abandon my sick children and my overwhelmed, grief-stricken husband. This was not a decision for me.

There were many days where the option of killing myself was what got me through one day of life. It is ironic that the thought of suicide could create one day of living. I didn't understand this logic, but I knew intuitively it was real, and on some level I knew others experienced this irony also. I eventually met others who also had the experience. We theorized it had something to do with being at the end with no options, and somehow having one last option is enough. Twisted but also sad and poignant. There are no words, no articles, no research studies, and no religion or prayers that can adequately describe the new normal left in the wake of our disastrous, violent, personal tsunami.

It defies logic, reason, and science, while it permanently alters the definition of family. We suffer a deep and chronic sorrow that comes with severe trauma. And in another twist of fate, my once powerful and steady voice, which advocated for mental health, was now but a whisper, and more often mute.

I completely understood the depth of our tragedy. I'd studied and worked in the field for over twenty-five years. I knew. Our fate, as it is for many, is worse than death; we now had four living bodies with four permanently and severely damaged brains.

Bipolar, in my opinion, is similar to other illnesses in severity, but it brings many obstacles and little to no compassion. No one brings dinner. There are no big national telethons, no community walk-a-thons, no celebrity fund raising. There is only isolation, stigma, and judgment.

Always stigma and judgment.

Chapter Fourteen

Kidnapped to the Other Side

I sobbed for hours and hours at a time, sometimes for days, and the days turned into weeks, and the weeks turned into months. Losing my children and getting sick was too much to handle on top of my tragic childhood. Finally, my husband insisted I spend some time in the hospital, as I could not stop crying from the dark depression and deep, agonizing grief. I experienced uncontrollable sobbing for four continuous months due to my first major depressive episode, post-traumatic stress, and a multi-sensory level of grief and loss that defies any experience I'd ever known in my life.

Signing into the hospital and providing specific details to a social worker was the first experience I had as a psychiatric patient. I spent many years working in mental health and I felt uneasy and afraid. Would I run into any psychiatrists I used to work with? Any that I currently shared cases with? Would I run into any clients? There were many things and people to fear.

But I respected my husband's opinion. I loved him and, more importantly, I trusted him. Truthfully, he needed a break from my grief.

He could not help himself, his children, or me. He was also grief-stricken. I could tell by the bags under his eyes and the lines on his handsome face that he was barely holding on as well. At that moment, I could not be the one to comfort him, as we both shared a moment in time that no couple or family should ever share.

And though I find men in general seem to like to fix things, this was a situation with no directions to follow where he was completely helpless. There was no medication for any of us to take in order to provide a quick fix for this mass onset of disease.

So I willingly signed myself into the hospital, having mixed feelings and a sense that this was not going to make me feel better. I went for my husband.

The majority of the clinical and technical staff acted as if the patients were invisible. They carried on personal conversations with their feet up, while sitting behind the nurse's station. Their conversations were about vacations, cars, and their weekend social events.

On occasion, they seemed to mock and sarcastically make fun of patients suffering with the most socially inappropriate symptoms. The clinicians and nurses lacked sophistication, were indifferent to the cruelty of their actions, and underestimated the insight of patients with active symptoms.

When patients approached the desk to either ask a question or request something, they were met with so-called professionals rolling their eyes, taking their time, and openly acting inconvenienced. I was not surprised, and I felt trapped and angry.

While patients with mostly bipolar disorder, major depression, schizoaffective disorder, and schizophrenia sat in a community room, the hospital employees insensitively acted as though none of us were present. We were unnoticeable and treated as if we had little to no human value. Their body language and laid back socializing spoke volumes that belied their training and desire to work in the healthcare field. It was incredibly rude and callous on every level.

The doctor assigned to my case was one I had worked with before as an addictions counselor. We were currently working with the same client who had a long history of co-occurring mental illnesses, including several lethal addictions, and we'd both met with her family on separate occasions. I had never met him in person. We'd only spoken on the telephone. When I met with him as a patient, at first he appeared to understand the gravity of my situation, my family history, the catastrophic story of my father, the heartbreaking story of my children's onset and severity of illness, and now my own.

He prescribed a couple of medications I was very familiar with and I refused to take due to extreme health risks and side effects. I had become educated about medication over the last few years trying to save my oldest daughter's life; therefore I imagined I would not be an easy patient to treat.

This was not grandiosity. We had our own clinical trial for years, with either success or failure as results. To physicians I likely lacked credibility on the issue of psychiatric medications, though living through horrific observations of my children suffering from occasional catastrophic medication trials. I was educated about pharmaceuticals. I was not trying to be difficult, though I'm sure he felt differently. Being difficult was now easier for me. Mental health workers had lied to us for years. No more.

On the third day of hospitalization, the psychiatrist did not try to hide his frustration with me and my refusal to take the medication he prescribed. He made an accusation that rocked me to the core.

"You must enjoy feeling this way since you keep refusing medication."

I was stunned and demoralized by his presumptuous and condemning statement. I explained to him that I'd read about the class action lawsuit, the risk for diabetes, the risk for blindness, and that I knew there were other medication choices.

What I didn't tell him was that I had met one of his other patients from his private practice who was also on the unit. He was a considerate gentleman who had taken the medication that I knew could cause diabetes and blindness. This gentleman had both side effects temporarily. His sight slowly returned in the short time that I was there, though, unconscionably, the staff did not give appropriate credence to his discomfort with the dayroom lighting. His experience confirmed what I already knew.

The psychiatrist discontinued our session abruptly and walked away without looking back. At first I felt insulted and hurt. That quickly turned to anger and resolve. No more.

The next morning the doctor came to get me again. I had spent the previous 24 hours attempting with little success to organize my very disorganized thoughts. I found it difficult, as my memory was not sequential, my thoughts were jumbled, and on occasion I was disoriented. What was clear was that my deep/dark depression and grief created a haze making it difficult to think and speak clearly and concisely.

However, I was determined. Underneath the illness, I was still there somewhere. I estimated I was most likely 90% unstable, so I relied on the 10% of brain cells still operational. I was hoping the brain cells that were working contained the parts of me that were assertive, compassionate, clinical to a degree, and, most importantly, the ones that held my emotional thoughts and feelings. The thoughts that I speak to convey the human experience. My own or someone else's. I was not sure which 10% was there. I took the chance. I had nothing left to lose.

We sat together in a little corner of the unit that offered no privacy. There was a small, round table between us and he was jotting some notes in a chart. I took a deep breath and began speaking in a hushed voice at first and very slowly. "I believe I have figured out, doctor, what is wrong with me and how you can help." The psychiatrist briefly glanced up at me from above his wire-rimmed glasses. His look was one of indifference. He continued to make notes. I imagined he was writing the same kind of thing about me that I might have written about patients decades ago when I worked for many years in an adolescent psychiatric hospital.

We were trained to use words like "resistant," "defiant," "oppositional," "non-compliant with treatment," "lacks respect for authority," and the one used most often that did not apply to me currently was "attention-seeking." It made me wonder if these children were seeking attention because of the pictures in their head or the noise in their ears. I felt so ashamed, but without training on brain disease and the focus always on behavioral health, how could I have known? I felt even sadder.

I brought my distant thoughts back to my current reality. I had already offered an opening statement, and, though he continued to write, I figured he had to listen to part of what I was saying since I only saw him for ten minutes daily. I couldn't imagine the reimbursement from my insurance company, but I was not in a position right now to think about that can of worms. I looked down at the carpet to try to focus and concentrate. I then found my voice and looked up directly into his indifferent eyes.

I spoke again. And this time I was going to finish and he was going to listen. "It's simple really. I have a broken heart. Shattered into small pieces and each piece is someone in my family." I paused and drew a deep breath and then continued. "You see I used to have an incredible life. A healthy and loving family. We played together and enjoyed simple things that brought us joy and a sense of completion to our lives. We had all of this in spite of our difficult childhoods.

"But now we are losing our beautiful children, all three in fact, as well as me, to the same disease that has already taken multiple family members.

"The same disease that killed my father and his innocent victims. The same disease that caused us public shame and humiliation. The same disease that gives reporters the *'right'* to speak badly of my sick family, using disrespectful names to describe people I love. Those of us, millions of us, who have little influence over our lives due to our brain disease, our neurological impairment, our cognitive deficits, or, as some like to label it, our mental illness.

"Do you have something for a mother's shattered heart? A daughter's dying heart? A sister's exhausted heart? How about a wife's grieving heart?

"Do you ever tell *lies in silence*?

"Have you ever been face to face in your home with what *lies in silence*?

"Has it snatched all the people you love?

"Can you fix me with medicine, give my children a normal life, and unravel and reverse this bipolar train wreck demolishing my entire family and every single person that I love?"

I took a breath, as it had been an exhausting effort to keep my thoughts sequential and clear so I could articulate them one by one. I knew it would be hard, but I did not realize the extent of the difficulty to explain or converse normally. I looked up at him again then and whispered while I looked into his dispassionate eyes.

"Can you?"

The tears came slowly down my face and he finally looked at me as if seeing me for the first time. No longer a mental patient. Finally a human being. He offered me a tissue.

He lowered his head, perhaps in shame, perhaps in sadness, and most hopefully in humility. He removed his glasses, put down his pen inside my chart, and looked into my sad and burdened eyes. It was his first direct look. He slowly shook his head no, and for the first time appeared like he was present in the moment. I continued.

"You really insulted me yesterday and your words and accusations were incredibly offensive. There is nothing, I assure you, about these symptoms that I enjoy, and what you said was cruel and judgmental, no different from the majority of the rest of the world. I was not expecting stigma from a psychiatrist, and I'm not sure I have faith in your ability to help me. You may feel frustrated with me, but you can never, in a million years, imagine how excruciating this illness is, and how with one fell swoop it knocks out an entire family unit. Unless of course you or someone you love has it.

"I'm used to being on the other side of the desk as a clinician. I am now a patient. Maybe you can work with me? I am educated, though I am very ill and grief-stricken. For the record, I won't ever take the two drugs you've prescribed and I have legitimate reasons. One I know is in a class action lawsuit due to several major medical issues reported in clinical trials and during current usage, and the other is highly addictive, something I would know about in my profession. If you'd like to discuss some other options, I am more than willing to listen."

After that morning, our conversations were professional, mutual, and respectful. I found myself distressed and upset, imagining many others judged for liking their symptoms and their illness. It made no sense to me, insulting and invalidating people when they are at their worst.

Looking at the other side of mental health was an eye-opener in such a negative and demoralizing way. I was ashamed for my profession and worried about the mental health care for my family.

One of the most confusing moments for me undoubtedly was the smoke break. I often elected to stay inside since I did not smoke, but there were a few patients who personally invited me to sit with them, mostly for company, as none of us were all that functional.

When it was time for a smoke break one of the judgmental unit staff would walk us down two flights of steps to a locked courtyard outside of the hospital. The patio was an older type of brick, the type used in historical buildings and some Victorian homes. It had a large green awning, like we were sitting at a pizzeria, with several round, wrought-iron tables, and plenty of matching chairs. There were ashtrays everywhere, and most patients chain-smoked while on the break.

Every time I agreed to join them, I had the exact same experience: I didn't know where to sit. From the very first break, I recognized clear identity confusion, as I was drawn to sit with the staff, as I did for 25 years as a clinician, though our definition of moral and ethical standards were obviously different. But this particular group of mental health workers made a clear and undeniable separation from the patients. So half of the time I sat with another patient and half of the time I stood staring at the massive concrete wall that faced the hospital and kept us prisoners. We were prisoners on a patio, prisoners on a psychiatric unit, prisoners of our brain chemistry and symptoms, and all taken hostage by mental illness. I was now kidnapped to the other side of the mental health profession, and I had plenty of company there. I stood at the wall alone, and though my thoughts continued to be loose and unclear, I knew exactly where I was and I knew exactly why. I imagined all of my family members standing at the wall at one time or another. Hand in hand stretched across the patio. We could fill an entire unit. This was a far cry from stretching hands across for a Sunday walk to the corner store. I quietly cried alone.

It was a crushing legacy. I was truly on the other side of the mental health system.

And the view was overwhelming.

Chapter Fifteen

So You Think You Know Mental Illness

A few weeks after being discharged from the hospital I heard from one of my sisters. The sister who had left home to be with a man in prison. A man she had never met in person.

The same sister who served time in jail when the man she had left home for was involved in an armed robbery. He was killed by the police, and she wound up serving time as an accessory. I only knew bits and pieces of the story because my mother kept it quiet. My sister had many years of suffering, including two failed marriages, untreated anxiety and panic attacks, unstable mood, and bulimia.

She had moved back and forth across the country several times. This was not a good sign, and it had bipolar written all over it. I was surprised to hear from her, as her contact over the years was sporadic at best.

She sent me an email sounding distraught and upset. Her daughter, my niece, had abruptly quit college, taken up with a man with a drug problem who was fifteen years older then she was, and they left the state together driving to some unknown location. I emailed her back immediately, and I attempted to explain the disease of bipolar disorder. The genetics. My children. Me.

But my sister was too ill and she was not interested in understanding the horrible genetic legacy of our family tree. She was rambling on and on and flatly denied that there was any mental illness in her family and certainly not her or her children.

She went on to describe things happening with her other child that were very distinct symptoms of unstable mood. There was no amount of educating that would open her mind to the possibility that there was something drastically wrong in her home.

More hostages for the mental illness death camp. The numbers were staggering. Multiple generations of one whole family.

My brother and other sister had both shown signs of a mood disorder early on, yet neither went for treatment. I long suspected they self-medicated in different ways, but they were secretive though their symptoms were quite obvious.

How many other families are eliminated from life in this manner?

I knew the number was in the millions. I felt overwhelmed as our numbers added up one by one.

For us, it was like a game of Jenga, removing one block at a time, anticipating the entire tower collapsing at some point. We were all blocks. I was staggered by the metaphor. We were in a full collapse without the opportunity to rebuild. The loss column was much longer by now. I tried to stop mentally adding them up one by one. There were too many.

It is alarming to me how many family members are now ill. I have come to accept that we will most likely experience suicide again, perhaps homicide, and most certainly public shame.

I have switched supermarkets to avoid questions about how my oldest child is doing in college and I avoid meeting the new neighbor across the street. It is predictable that the police will be at our home again forcibly taking someone to the crisis center. These horrific possibilities are inevitable and unpredictable. It is like living with a bomb where all of the wires are connected, and the timer is counting down, waiting for the next devastating explosion.

Chapter Sixteen

Continuing Heartbreak

After much angst and discussion, we told our oldest daughter if she left in the middle of the night again, she could not come back. She left anyway. She and her mental illness. It was ten days before her high school graduation, and my heart had now stopped beating, as it kept being ripped right out of my chest, and we struggled to get through what there is no map for.

Many days afterwards, she began incessantly calling her dad's cell phone, all through the afternoon and into the early evening. On one of the few occasions I picked up the phone, she immediately started petitioning me to let her return home.

My husband began to question our decision as she cried, "I have nowhere to go." He turned to me and sadly said, "I don't know what to do. What are we supposed to do? This is our child. How do we manage this?"

I've had some clinical training and years of counseling families with dually diagnosed teens, so this decision, though not a simple one, was easier for me to hold firm on than it was for him. I decided I would not push my agenda. If in fact she died in the process, he would blame me. Our marriage was under enough strain with the amount of mental illness and difficulty we faced daily.

I had to work that night and I did not get home until well after 9:00 PM. I was still masquerading as a professional though my personal life had become a tragedy.

When I came home, my husband informed me he had changed his mind. He no longer felt obligated to allow her back into our home. He gave no reason for his change of heart. However, when she started calling on all the phones we own, he made no motion to answer them.

Avoidance was his current tactic. Since there is no way to parent a mentally ill child, much like trying to reason with a parent who has dementia, we would sometimes have a plan and eventually throw it out the window. This was brain damage. Nothing makes sense, and you have to live it to get it.

A few hours later, we heard a car at the top of the driveway. It was well after midnight. She shook every door (locks changed), she went into the car looking for the garage door opener (we took it), and then she started to call relentlessly. I had a flashback to the day the reporters started to call our house and I was told not to answer the phone. I chose that option at first but eventually picked up the receiver. This call was not a reporter. This call was our unstable daughter. Different circumstances, decades apart, but still driven by the force of what *lies in silence*.

After some brief, circular, and random conversations on the phone, she walked up to the front porch. The same front porch where her journey seemed to begin, on a late evening in the middle of our street. I cracked the heavy, wooden front door open and peered through the screen. She stood a few feet away with her arms folded. It was raining lightly.

"I'm going to call the police," I told her. My tactic was to push her emotionally. This was a dance we used to do when she was mentally healthy and bottled everything up. It usually worked before bipolar disorder stole her mind. I figured I had nothing to lose.

We had called the state police three previous times to get her to the crisis center. There was always something going on outside, which made the situation worse. On a couple of occasions, three squad cars came together, one right after the other pulling down into our driveway. At the same time, the afternoon school buses rolled by. Once our next-door neighbor, who was picking up his mail, glanced over with a confused look on his face. These were wonderful neighbors, where we took turns dog sitting for one another and borrowed things easily back and forth. They never asked and we never told.

These memories flooded back to me as I watched her. I had no idea of how this would play out. She was not in the driver's seat of her sense and sensibility.

I told her she no longer had a home. I told her to call her friends since they take better care of her. I told her to call a shelter and see if there was a bed. The more I talked, the more she wept. After hollering about some nonsensical stuff, she somehow organized her thoughts and reached down deeply into the core of her soul. I watched this while a deep burn shot through my heart and the backs of my eyes grew heavy with unshed tears.

Her crying turned into deep and piercing sobs. Though unstable and standing in the rain, she found her voice while standing in the dark, locked out of what had been her home, as I watched and listened from the foyer.

It felt like a scene out of a dramatic film, the type of film that predictably has a sad ending. A film where you fall in love with the characters over and over and what they mean to one another. Classic films, where you emotionally prepare yourself for the tragic ending, but cry each and every time you watch. And you watch it repeatedly because it is about human connection and emotional intimacy.

This was our family film. Our film of love, our film of characters, our film about a tragic journey and an unchangeable ending.

My daughter found her voice but struggled to organize her thoughts in the middle of an aggressive episode. She spoke through buckets and buckets of tears, choking and gulping in an attempt to rid herself of pent up emotion — emotion that no adolescent has language, words, insight, or critical thinking ability to express in a manner that makes sense. I felt flushed and helpless. I knew what was coming, though unprepared for how well organized and connected her thoughts and feelings were. She knew all along but could not say. Speaking the words only confirmed what she was already living. She knew it and so did we.

She took a deep breath of cold, damp air and stared in my direction.

"I AM ANGRY BECAUSE I HAVE TO LIVE HERE! I AM ANGRY BECAUSE I AM SUPPOSED TO BE IN COLLEGE! I GOT ACCEPTED, YOU KNOW! I WORKED REALLY HARD TO GET ACCEPTED TO THAT UNIVERSITY, MOM. I STUDIED HARD, AND I GOT HONOR ROLL GRADES, AND SCORED OVER 1100 ON MY SATS!!

"I AM ANGRY BECAUSE PEOPLE SCREW ME OVER!! I AM ANGRY BECAUSE I HAVE THIS F---ING DISEASE!!! I AM ANGRY BECAUSE YOU AND DADDY KNEW WE WOULD GET SICK! I DON'T UNDERSTAND WHY YOU HAD CHILDREN WHEN YOUR FATHER AND SISTER HAD BEEN SO SICK!!

I HAD A GREAT LIFE UNTIL THIS DISEASE!! NOW I HAVE NOTHING!!! NONE OF THE THINGS YOU SAID I COULD HAVE!! YOU TOLD ME IF I TOOK MEDS AND GOT HELP I'D FEEL BETTER!! I DON'T!! EVERYONE

LIED TO ME!! AND WORSE THAN ANYTHING, YOU AND
DADDY LIED TO ME!!!!"

I had a flashback to the scene in the church. I was told my dad
was screaming at our minister looking for someone to blame.

He was saying the same things. They were both telling the
truth.

I just stood there, numb and paralyzed, peering through my
locked screen door while she cried and cried. The losses never go
away. Never. They add up and now they seemed to multiply yet
again.

We discussed some minor issues before I let her into the house
under the stipulation that nothing was different yet. She said, "I
want everything to be normal and like it used to be."

I said, "Me, too, honey, but it won't. It won't ever be that way
again. The love and simple fun we once had is almost impossible
to maintain with the majority of us having mood disorders. Fair?
No. Truth? Yes."

She said, "You know, mom, things don't always happen for a
reason like people say."

I said, "I know. I have learned that lesson also, many times, I
am afraid to say. Many, many times."

She came into the kitchen and we continued some light
conversation. I brought up some old concerns. She responded to
them, "I have smoked pot to get some sleep, but it usually made

me really paranoid. So, I drink alcohol more often because it numbs the physical and emotional pain, and at least I get some sleep. I can't sleep without a lot of medication and alcohol is just easier to get."

Ah, truth at last. I told her I could handle the information, and that, even though I was her mom, who else to tell this crap to than a bipolar, drug-and-alcohol-counseling mother. Ironic and so horribly unjust and sad.

I asked her if she needed a hug. She sobbed and sobbed in my arms and buried her face in my neck. Another one of my children seeking comfort in my neck.

We stood there for what seemed like hours but was only minutes. A moment in time when we shared our grief for the present, and a joint acknowledgement of the magnitude of what we had lost and were continuing to lose. And then there were more difficult questions being asked. Our family now had three generations seeking answers to questions.

"I don't understand. Why did you and dad have children?"

I took a deep breath. At the same moment tears welled up in my eyes again. She was asking me the same question my father asked. My mother asked. I asked. And now she asked.

Why was there no public information about the likelihood of a genetic predisposition?

If we were so aptly warned about heart disease, cancer, and high blood pressure, why not mental illness?

I spoke quietly so she could genuinely listen. "We did not know. There were no warnings. No words of caution. No percentage of risk. Nothing. Only *lies in silence*."

She looked at me shaking her head. "I don't believe you. How is that possible?"

I took her face in my hands and said tearfully, "You really did get a raw deal. I get that. You are very young to suffer like this. I'm so sorry. If you want help trying to get better, then we'll help. It's your brain, your life, and your pain. I get it. But we really didn't know. No one knew. Only silence. Deafening silence."

"Mom, if you and daddy knew back then, would you have had children?"

Thinking to myself there must be a questioning gene, I let out a long sigh and proceeded. "At the very least we would have been able to make an informed decision. Given the information we have now, I would have to say it is unlikely. I hope that makes sense to you."

I started to cry harder as this was the first time I had answered that question honestly, and I felt like a horrible mother saying it to my daughter. She told me not to cry. Then we laughed because she said she couldn't get any antipsychotics or mood stabilizers on the street and she was up for many nights... dark bipolar humor.

Her manic episodes got much harder to manage, as the highly disordered thinking seemed to border on delusional. Screaming things like, "You don't love me. You never have. You love everybody else better than me." Statements with no real basis. Sad for any parent to hear and experience after years of sacrifice raising a child. Years of beautiful memories. Years of dreams and hopes.

This was sad. Just sad. Incomprehensible loss, served with unending judgment. A permanent hole in my spirit and soul. A mother's loving, but now shattered, soul.

During one of her episodes, we tried to convince her to voluntarily admit herself to a hospital. She reluctantly agreed, so we cleared the schedule, got two family members to stay with the other kids, and drove to the ER.

We knew it was going to be a bad outcome when she refused at first to sign the consent for an evaluation. After being seen by a physician and a social worker, they informed us that she denied being suicidal. She had called that weekend twice. Once at 4:30 AM and the following morning at 5:00 AM.

Both times, she was sobbing and begging for help, talking about suicide. She denied this to the clinicians.

The social worker approached us with a strange look on his face. He had close-cropped hair, stood rather tall, wearing khaki pants, expensive brown loafers, and a blue Oxford button-down shirt. He appeared as though he may have just finished graduate school at an Ivy League campus, and I could sense he was going to share some of his expensive education with us. I guessed there was an age difference in clinical and life experience of about two decades. I inhaled and exhaled as deeply as possible. My gut told me we were going to have a *discussion*. I was in no mood to have a clinical discussion with this opinionated, book-smart, rookie professional. Poor guy didn't even see it coming.

The social worker informed us of the news that as an adult she had to give her consent to treatment unless she met criteria for a commitment (things I have practiced for years). He went on to say, "You know some people have to reach rock bottom before they seek help."

I felt the blood rise in my face and I knew the unlucky fellow was at the wrong place, at the wrong time, talking to the wrong woman. Thankfully, we were sitting as he stood over us.

I looked at him and started slowly,

"With all due respect, sir, are you yourself mentally ill?

"Do you by chance have a mentally ill child?

"Perhaps a mentally ill parent or sibling?

"Do you live with someone who is mentally ill?"

He went to speak and I cut him off. My blood was now at a boil.

"Do you have a family history of completed suicide?

"Do you have a family history of completed homicide?

"That IS our family's bottom. We'll bring her back in a body bag and perhaps then you'll treat her. Until you can speak with any amount of knowledge, don't quote us the company line and impress us with what you have read in a book."

At that point, my husband got up from the chair where he'd been sitting next to me with his head in both palms. It was apparent I had lost some control, since my words were becoming more heated and more pointed.

He stood up at the right time, as I was organizing the next part of my speech that included asking him if he had any family member put a loaded gun to his head.

Our daughter agreed to blood work, which we assumed was for STDs and pregnancy. Once she got the results, she refused treatment. We left the ER and took her back to the dangerous area where she was living. At first she refused to get out of the car. We were confused, but of course illness was in charge. Maybe she had wanted the blood test and then the chance to return to our home? Trying to guess with mental illness is an often-futile game. We told her she could not come home since she refused treatment. She got out of the car, cursed us out, and made some inappropriate hand gestures. That was not our daughter.

Even though we tried, it still wasn't possible for our daughter to live with us. It was simply too chaotic and too dangerous for our other children. So now she lives on the street or moves from house to house, as well as losing one job after another.

She refuses to sign herself into a treatment center and goes off of her medication for months at a time. Her distorted reasoning is that she was still sick when taking twelve pills a day. She was. She insists that she is an adult and cannot be admitted without voluntary consent.

She is unable to manage any type of lifestyle, and though, when medicated her brain and her thoughts quiet down some, there are many things that happen that feel very much like *déjà vu*. She cannot follow simple rules and has escalated her alcohol intake to the point of blacking out.

She's becoming a combination of my father, my siblings, and many of my clients. She's entering the world of dual diagnosis, where the prognosis gets worse, where competent treatment services are unavailable or inaccessible, and very few counselors truly understand the significant interplay of symptom presentation. They do not grasp how the unstable mood drives the substance abuse and the substances damage the brain and other parts of the body, creating physical complications. Many of them recommend linear interventions (perhaps 12-step meetings or only medication as individual treatment) to handle the entire complicated picture, rather than a more comprehensive plan that includes co-occurring and sophisticated treatment provided by multiple competent providers.

So, we stumble through our sad and tragic life, attempting to find ways to live with no roadmap, no guidance, and no long-term, effective treatment.

And still I find myself with questions. Lots of questions.

Questions that no one likes to ask.

Questions that no one likes to answer.

Questions that may be politically incorrect for some.

Questions that mental health professionals may think to themselves but rarely speak.

Questions that may insult those who are mentally ill, high functioning, and living fairly normal lives, with a career and successful relationships. The small percentage of those would be some of the last people to ask or answer these questions. As this is a spectrum disorder, there are people all over the spectrum. In addition, as we can recognize some people suffer less, we must also recognize the landscape has now changed.

This disease is not kind to adults. And it is even less kind to children, whose suffering may likely never allow them to live a close to normal lifestyle. Many children. Not just some. Research says millions.

It is time to have multiple discussions about this.

There are so many more questions in addition to the ones I've asked already.

If bipolar disorder is a highly genetic family illness, why is there no family treatment?

Why are mental illness and addiction excluded in genetics counseling both before and after conception?

Is it possible there is a connection between the emergence and drastic increase in school shootings and earlier onset of mental illness?

Is it possible there is a connection between lower ages of onset of substance abuse, as young as elementary school age, and mental illness?

If we improved our mental health care and put more money into research, rather than the mental health arena remaining an unyielding afterthought, would we finally address other chronic life-threatening, family-threatening, and community-threatening issues?

Why must we beg for parity with a disease of the brain? Is it not a journey parallel to the fight for the right of all citizens to vote?

Why is the committee that is working on the DSM-V, the diagnostic statistical manual, uncertain about the inclusion of early onset (pediatric) bipolar disorder as a legitimate illness?

Does this committee fail to recognize how this exclusion invalidates the daily living hell of families?

Moreover, without a doubt, my most controversial and politically incorrect question by far:

If hypersexuality is a persistent and chronic symptom of some mental illnesses, should we not carefully research if there is a correlation to the epidemic of sexual abuse, sexual addictions, and pornography addiction?

Do we have the scientific methods for this type of research?

Would we not best serve the public with updated mental health services, rather than shaming sick people on prime time television?

What will it be like watching my three children slip away from my heart?

Chapter Seventeen

New "Normal"

Simple things in our life are no longer simple. I can feel the changes in my brain. Things like initiation and motivation are missing. Taking a shower, washing the dishes, doing laundry, giving my child a bath, and even changing my own clothes are no longer a natural part of my life. Things that used to be routine are now difficult and tedious.

In order to accomplish things I have to set small goals and then internally talk my way through them. It is embarrassing and I feel ashamed that I can't organize and clean the house in the manner I used to.

On occasion, having the desire to be productive in spite of my disoriented brain, I venture toward the laundry room in an attempt to do some laundry. Many times on that brief walk, I forget what I am doing and begin to straighten pillows or pick lint up from the carpet. If I can then recall, I go back toward the original task of doing laundry, while whispering to myself, "I can't believe I am now mentally ill. How will I ever get anything done like this?"

Never thinking I would feel this way: I miss cleaning, I miss dusting, and, unbelievably, I miss doing the toilets. I had taken these simple acts for granted and disliked them like everyone else. Until now.

Though I was unable to cook for a long while, eventually that skill returned, once I started medication. The other simple tasks sadly have not come back.

I have lost interest in reading and going to the library, lost interest in our swim club, and cannot seem to get back any portion of our normal existence due to biochemical obstacles as well as psychosocial ones.

I miss our old life. I miss my old self. I miss my children. The losses continue to mount. I ache for what my children must be experiencing, as I can barely handle this as an educated adult.

They look to me and their dad for answers and comfort. Nothing has been more painful than losing my children and watching their suffering while others lack compassion, understanding, and tolerance.

I try to explain to those that foolishly think they understand this illness that there are limited states of mind. One is full-blown instability, where the symptoms are present and preventing function. Another is full stability, or stability with some breakthrough symptoms such as anxiety, sleep disturbance, or other symptoms present even while medicated and mostly stable. During periods of stability there is no escape from the sorrow, the grief, and the chronic suffering of a life that is forever changed.

Crisis calls. Psychiatric appointments. Insulting professionals that feel the need to try out their book knowledge. Long-time friends dropping out of our life. Others judging our parenting. Stupid questions. Catastrophic medication reactions. Loss of loving family relationships. Loss of dreams. Loss of simple joys like holding hands, sitting by a warm campfire under the bright moon, discovering a new type of tree, or sharing a conversation while sipping a cup of hot apple spice tea. Gone.

Life is now robotic and lacks the deeper joy and comfort it once had.

Our home is in disrepair, as we fall behind in routine maintenance. Our basement, though partially finished, is not completely done, and there is a reminder daily of how our lives now stand still, as my husband completed a beautiful brick front walkway that leads to a cement slab for what was to be our new front porch. A walkway meant to be friendly and welcoming to those entering our family home.

Our back deck, built several years ago, needs boards replaced and a fresh coat of stain. These and many other projects were abruptly and forcefully halted by the unwelcome guest of severe, chronic, and persistent neurobiological disease.

The roof on our home has needed replacement since the massive onset of mental illness. It took the kitchen ceiling crashing in to force us to make the decision to replace it, even though there was a possibility of being short on money to pay medical and pharmaceutical bills.

In addition, the kitchen and the bathrooms, which we wanted to remodel, most certainly will remain the same. They will stay as they were in the era that was long before we knew what and who *lies in silence.* Ironically my father's era.

The war is over. And though it is controversial to admit it, I can only hope now that my children do not have children of their own. If they do, we will lose more young hostages that will not be safe in their brain, in their family, potentially in their school and in their community. The loss of being a grandmother is a sacrifice I am willing to make so I don't have to watch another generation suffer unduly. In spite of that desire, our oldest daughter got pregnant during a manic episode, and there is now a fourth generation of illness. She continues to live house to house or in shelters, now hypocritically passing the genetics to another life to be lost. Her illness tricked her into thinking she would be a better parent. Were it not for mental illness I would be deeply insulted. Instead I am traumatized that there is another child that will suffer, and I cannot bring myself to become involved in another catastrophic situation. The one I have is more than I can handle.

In our family clinical trial, we are 100%. That is more than enough information for me. I no longer need the genetics researchers to tell me the obvious. I can tell them. I wonder if they will listen.

I will be the one who offers my children the genetics counseling I never received. I will tell them to look at the percentage of family members with bipolar and other serious co-occurring disorders, so they can make an informed decision based on that. Something I wish someone had told me. Anyone.

I no longer have faith in humanity because stigma, criticism, and ignorance run deep. I no longer have faith in the medical community, because of their silence, and I am overwhelmed with the lack of urgency around mental health in our country.

As we wait longer and longer to create effective, thoughtful, and efficient ways to slay this type of illness, it is evident to me that it will continue to reveal itself in every community. Bipolar will continue to affect people of all backgrounds, create suffering, and confuse the public in general with its cunning silence by creating the distraction and illusion of other's lies.

What sadly lives in many families *lies in silence*.

Lies In Silence

It is watching my beautiful, talented children
slowly lose themselves,
their spirit, and their dreams to this disease
I question what
Lies In Silence?

It is when we look over our medical expenses,
the amount of time and money spent on treatment
with no long-term relief
I question what
Lies In Silence?

It is when I worry I'll become a "mentally unstable"
burden on my husband,
rather than his loving partner in life
I question what
Lies In Silence?

It is when I crush an atypical antipsychotic
into applesauce, pudding, or yogurt
for my beautiful hazel, curly-haired toddler
I question what
Lies In Silence?

It is when I sign involuntarily,
my once loving and intelligent daughter
into a psychiatric unit,
rather than admitting her to her first choice university
I question what
Lies In Silence?

It is when I read my father's name,
fully and correctly spelled,
in a magazine or newspaper
I question who
Lies In Silence?

It is when I feel sick to my stomach
as I drive by our old church,
the place that used to be a haven for my family and me
I question what
Lies In Silence?

It is when I review old email or
professional notes that I have written,
and they make no sense
I question what
Lies In Silence?

It is when I am too sick to plan a birthday party,
a holy communion,
or a traditional holiday dinner
I question what
Lies In Silence?

It is when I can only work part time,
in a career that took decades to build,
with a graduate degree,
and extensive clinical training and supervision
I question what
Lies In Silence?

It is when my hands tremble and shake
and my clothes no longer fit,

because of side effects from medication
I question what
Lies In Silence?

It is when we have to sell our quaint retirement cottage,
we bought only a few years ago
I question what
Lies In Silence?

It is when our daughter, a talented athlete, sits in the house
all summer long, suffering from a deep depression,
while her friends play outside and go to sports camp
I question what
Lies In Silence?

It is when I see the pained and vacant look
in my husband's sad eyes,
as he drops me off at a psychiatric hospital
I question what
Lies In Silence?

It is when my oldest daughter is on the run for weeks,
refusing meds and spending time with people
who seem to have their own mental health problems
I question what
Lies In Silence?

It is when I look at all of the human loss,
the relationship and family loss,
the future that was, and the loss of simple, joyful daily living
I SCREAM WHAT
Lies In Silence?

Chapter Eighteen

Who Will Answer My Questions?

And I have even more pressing, provocative, and potentially offensive questions.

As we watch the suicide rate climb, the murder rate climb, and violence in our communities rise, are we looking at the possible connection to untreated, treatment-resistant, or mistreated mental illness?

As teen pregnancy and sexually transmitted diseases rise in certain cultures, and gun violence is at an epidemic proportion, are we looking to the possible connection to untreated, treatment-resistant, or mistreated mental illness?

As the abuse of drugs and alcohol rise in addition to increases of all addictions: gambling, shopping, food, and sex, I can't help but to wonder, is there a relationship between these statistics, these behaviors, these severe chronic issues, and untreated, treatment-resistant, or mistreated mental illness?

Is anyone paying attention to what seem to be prominent trends?

We are building bigger prisons to accommodate the growing population of inmates. The overcrowding is chronic and mental health services for prisoners are substandard, if they even exist.

While building larger prisons, we are closing psychiatric hospitals, residential treatment programs, rehabilitation centers, and making treatment more difficult to obtain.

We have a tremendous shortage of pediatric psychiatrists in this country, as third party reimbursement withholds dollars; malpractice insurance is not within reach for some, and the genetics of mental illness marches on, increasing waiting lists with desperate patients living with desperate family members.

If we are to focus on HIV and childhood illnesses like autism, shouldn't we also investigate vigorously whether mental illness plays a key role in some of the biggest sociological, financial, medical, and psychological issues of our time?

If the psychiatric community continues to fight among themselves about pediatric bipolar, how do we diagnose children?

Where do we place two-, three-, or four-year-old, mentally ill children who threaten their families with knives?

Why would any family seek education or treatment for their children with grossly diseased brains, when uneducated celebrities discredit and invalidate mental illness and its legitimate existence?

Some may disagree with my questions or my thoughts, but I believe in the wise saying, "You shouldn't judge another until you've walked a mile in their shoes." Do you walk with the mentally ill?

Through my personal life, as well as my professional life, I believe I have some possible answers. Conclusions that are mine alone.

Many professionals and politicians have not solved these riddles nor answered these questions. They are asking the wrong questions. Therefore, the answers do not have value in moving us toward solutions. So we're stuck. All of us.

My answers have come the hard way. I feel dismayed. I am disappointed. And I live in fear, for how much longer this emerging epidemic can go on before getting the attention it needs.

Who and what *lies in silence* may be one of the most threatening and menacing domestic terrors we have. Silent and invisible, it lies in slumber, waiting for its next opportunity to strike.

I was not prepared. My family was not prepared. It is a looming and present crisis.

In my opinion, our research is decades behind. No one has legitimized the genetic connections sufficiently, and we lack resources at every level to help families like mine.

I recognize that there is more open discussion on mental illness and the use of medication. But there are still millions who suffer. Both current and future couples making plans for a family need much more accurate information.

Restrictive insurance policies dictate treatment based on dollars, not disease. We need user-friendly and consistent federal parity law, an easy process in place to get medical assistance, and procedures to quickly and efficiently obtain pharmaceuticals. We need solutions to treat and quiet our raging children. No police calls. No holes in the wall. If for only one night your child's brain can experience silence, her soul not feel possessed, and his spirit not be lifeless and dead.

We may never tackle mental illness until we stop using terms like *crazy* to describe the mentally ill or *crack head* to describe someone struggling with a horribly addicting drug, possibly taken as self-medication for mental illness.

As I review our journey as a family, most days I am overwhelmed with grief. It is the big things and the little things. And regardless whether the symptoms are quiet or loud, it is never far from my mind that these diseases are winning. My entire family has lost.

They have stolen from me my childhood, my children, my father, my sisters, my brothers, uncles, and cousins. They have robbed me of my dignity, extinguished my spirit, and erased my hope and faith, leaving us with a future that was.

Bipolar and co-occurring disorders are catastrophic, unforgiving, multi-generational illnesses similar to muscular dystrophy, Huntington's disease, and cancer in magnitude, death, destruction, and, most significantly, genetics.

Those who don't know it personally or through a close family member they live with can never, ever understand the enormity of the loss and suffering.

Like a terrorist seeking to destroy innocent citizens, a natural disaster of immense scope, or a tragedy of unthinkable proportions, bipolar and other mental illnesses wipe out dreams, goals, family units, and human souls.

We are on a slippery slope that lets us have the privilege of living as an insane, free American yet lacking access to treatment. De-institutionalization, a failed attempt to resolve one major issue, inadvertently caused a multitude of other issues in a chronically ineffective mental health system. A system that does not meet the needs of many Americans. Some believe this has become one of our most shameful legacies, in addition to a few others.

There is a deficiency of education in the medical arena in terms of information that is useful and authentic. Without ongoing competent clinical supervision, it is a vicious cycle of teaching useless interventions. Though most understand that offering counseling to a patient in the middle of a seizure is ineffective, the same professionals do not translate that understanding to diseases of the brain. They lack updated education about potentially mood-triggering medications, and I imagine few providers are even asking about family history.

There is a lack of understanding of the lethal implications of prescribing medicines such as steroids, calcium channel blockers, antidepressants, and stimulants with often-tragic consequences.

There is a lackadaisical mentality about the potential to destroy children, adolescents, adults, and families who are already predisposed to the genetics of unstable mood.

We are lacking in mental health education in the legal system, and there is little to no interest in creating appropriate mental health laws.

My family lost everything: some because of this lack of education, some because of the lack of updated and comprehensive genetics counseling, some because of the stigma that creates a deafening silence.

Bipolar: a serious and chronic brain disorder took everything. There is nothing left to take.

I started to think about how I would explain this in simple terms. Many have asked:

What is life like now?

How do you get through the days?

Some of us that live this way call it the art of masquerade.

masquerade: 1 a: to disguise oneself; also: to go about disguised; b: to take part in a masquerade 2: to assume the appearance of something one is not

When I discuss a day in the life with those who are in my inner circle of trust, we all understand and live the "masquerade." Whether it is attending a family function, or picking out a dress for a dance, or showing up for work regardless of symptoms and burdens at home, it is a "masquerade" in order to get through a day. When asked. "How was your weekend?" the answer is fine, though the truth is unlikely that it was fine. When asked, "How are the kids?" the answer is "fine." It is a short word and moves things along. Nothing is fine, and will never again be fine, though we "masquerade" as though it is.

And although I have always had some level of belief in formal religion, I have more so been a spiritual person.

A woman full of life, kind in disposition,

loving, giving, and always optimistic.

I now question daily, my faith

and the future for my husband,

my children, and myself. So I stay in

the moment. Never tomorrow.

Only now.

Because now may be all we have as a family.

Ever.

The only hope I cling to, desperately,

is that what

Lies In Silence

does not lie in eternity.

Resources

The National Suicide Prevention Lifeline is a 24-hour, toll-free suicide prevention service available to anyone in suicidal crisis. If you need help, please dial 1-800-273-TALK (8255). You will be routed to the closest possible crisis center in your area.
http://www.suicidepreventionlifeline.org

Depression and Bipolar Support Alliance (DBSA). Along with proper diagnosis and treatment, the support of others is vital to a lifetime of wellness. Take the next step toward wellness for you or someone you love. Visit www.DBSAlliance.org/findsupport or call 800-826-3632 to find the group nearest you. If there's not a support group in your community, DBSA can help you start one.

Education and training programs receiving funds from the author:

Coppin State University — Department of Social Work
2500 West North Avenue
Baltimore, MD 21216-3698
1-800 635-3674 ext. 3802, webmaster@coppin.edu

Thomas Jefferson University Medical School and Research Department
of Psychiatry & Human Behavior
The Bipolar Education and Research Fund
833 Chestnut East — Suite 210A
Philadelphia, PA 19107-5587
215-955-8570

SJ Hart will be establishing a program that addresses the needs in the Hispanic community, in recognition of the increase in numbers of suicides and lack of easy access to treatment. She is currently negotiating with several non-profit organizations focused on mental illness, substance abuse, and cultural obstacles in the Hispanic community in Southern California.

167

Glossary

antidepressants medicines used to treat depression and other illnesses.

bipolar I disorder a type of bipolar disorder where a person has one or more episodes of mania or mixed mood episodes. The person also may have one or more episodes of major depression.

bipolar II disorder a type of bipolar disorder where a person has one or more episodes of major depression and hypomania.

cognitive-behavioral therapy a type of talk therapy that helps people identify and change ways of thinking that are not helpful to them.

cyclothymic disorder a mood disturbance where there are repeated periods of mild depression and normal or slightly elevated moods.

depression (or depressive episode or major depressive episode) a period of at least two weeks in which a person feels very sad, lacks energy, is not interested in usual activities, and may feel like things are hopeless. Often the person isn't able to function normally.

hypomania (or hypomanic episode) a condition similar to mania, but not as severe. A person has a high mood and may behave strangely. But the person is able to function normally.

maintenance therapy treatment to prevent or delay the symptoms of a medical condition. Medicines can be a kind of maintenance therapy. People with bipolar disorder usually need to keep taking medicines even after they feel better.

mania (or manic episode) a period of time where a person is very happy, irritable, or reckless. The person isn't able to function normally. In severe cases, the person may see or hear things that are not really there.

manic depression an older name for bipolar disorder.

mixed episode when symptoms of mania and depression happen every day for at least a week.

mood chart a chart for recording emotions and important life events.

mood disorder a mental disorder connected with a disturbed mood, such as bipolar disorder.

mood stabilizers medicines that can help balance a person's mood.

neurotransmitter a chemical that sends messages from one brain cell to another.

psychiatrist a medical doctor who specializes in treating mental and emotional disorders. Psychiatrists can prescribe medicines and provide talk therapy.

psychiatry a branch of medicine that deals with mental, emotional, or behavioral problems.

psychologist a healthcare professional who treats mental or emotional disorders.

psychology the scientific study of mind and behavior.

psychotherapy a way of treating a mental or emotional disorder by regularly talking with a doctor or therapist. Also known as "talk therapy" or counseling.

rapid cycling having at least four episodes of manic, mixed, hypomanic, or depressive episodes in a year.

triggers events, either good or bad, that might cause a mood swing. Also called stressors.

SJ Hart is available for public speaking and cross-industry clinical training on mental health issues. She can be contacted through Idyll Arbor (sales@IdyllArbor.com or 360-825-7797).

A portion of the author's income from *Lies In Silence* book sales and speaking engagements is being donated toward research and treatment for Bipolar and Co-occurring Disorders.

CPSIA information can be obtained
at www.ICGtesting.com
Printed in the USA
FFOW02n2242090118
44454865-44248FF